# THE KEY TO THE KEY

Throughout The Key you will see different symbols with instructions. Here is 'your key to The Key' so that you know what to do:

- 🔑 **Write your thoughts**
- ▶ **Watch video.** Go to www.romigrossberg.com/the-key
- ↻ **Answer the re-cap questions to show your understanding**
- ✎ **Scribble some thoughts or doodle if you like**
- 🏠 **Homework**
- ⚡ **Activity**

# THE KEY

My name is _____

I am in year _____ at _____ (school name).

Today I am _____ years, _____ months and _____ days

on _____ day _____ month _____ year.

# CONTENTS

The key to The Key ................................................................... 1
The Author ............................................................................. 7
The Key .................................................................................. 10

## SECTION ONE - MY FRIENDSHIPS                             15
What Kind of Friend Are You? ................................................ 22
Jealousy & Envy .................................................................... 26
Bullies .................................................................................... 33
Story Time ............................................................................. 38
Apologies ............................................................................... 42
Compliments ......................................................................... 45
Values .................................................................................... 48
Empathy ................................................................................. 52
'My Friendships' Wrap Up ..................................................... 59

## SECTION TWO - ME                                                     61
Tone of voice ......................................................................... 71
Choice .................................................................................... 75
Breath .................................................................................... 90
Anxiety ................................................................................... 92
Success & Failure .................................................................. 96
Unconditional Love ............................................................. 103
Negative Thoughts ............................................................... 106
Creating Positive Affirmations ............................................. 111
Sadness Versus Happiness .................................................. 119
Depression .......................................................................... 126
'Me' Wrap Up ....................................................................... 129

## SECTION THREE - MY FAMILY                                  131
My Home .............................................................................. 139
Divorce ................................................................................. 142
Finding the Good ................................................................. 146
'My Family' Wrap Up ........................................................... 147
Going Forward ..................................................................... 149
Acknowledgements ............................................................. 153

"Teenagers are often tense and anxious, which leaves them particularly vulnerable to making bad decisions or exhibiting risky behaviours.

The Key is designed to help young people explore their own values and insecurities and to give them essential tools and coping mechanisms, such as self-reflection, time management, and positive self-talk to decrease the effects of stress and conflict in their daily lives.

This interactive self-help book takes a concise and cool-headed look at some of the most important stress points in a teenager's life: Friendships, Me, and My Family.

The Key is very readable. (Romi) Grossberg addresses her teenage audience in a language that is unpatronizing while presenting complex issues and concepts with exceptional clarity.

The Key never offers bland, "look on the bright side" advice. Grossberg delivers a series of common-sense self-care strategies in a clear and comforting manner designed to help put adolescent problems in perspective. Moreover, she provides her readers with the strategies for practical problem-solving and finding solutions to stressful situations. The author also gives teenagers terrific tips on becoming more balanced and goal-oriented. As the readers navigate the activities they can come to powerful and meaningful decisions and take greater control of their lives.

I wish I had read this when I was a teenager, it may have helped.

Highly recommended."

**Kevin Morley**
Author (Oxford University Press).
Independent Education Consultant
Teacher and Teacher Trainer.


"I wish I had The Key in my teenage years. It is a fascinating and engaging program, skillfully designed to reach the most critical participants in the world: teenage students - and it does a brilliant job doing so. 'The Key' is teaching young people fundamental and actionable steps to raise their emotional intelligence - a central and learnable skill which enhances all other skills. As a psychotherapist I know a lot of my clients would have enormously profited from a training like this in their early years, saving them years of suffering. From a psychological point of view it seems critical for the future of our society to implement programs like this in our school system. If you have responsibility for teenagers and want them to prosper in life, this is the book for you!"

**Zoltan Gal**
Master in Psychology; Master in Philosophy.
Psychotherapist, Head of the Psychosomatic Institute in Munich, Germany.

"Today's teens are anxious and stressed. The pressure to keep up - both in school and online - has led to a mounting mental health crisis in schools and universities worldwide. It's clear we need to take a preventative approach, one that will help our students find healthy ways to cope. Social and emotional learning provides the framework to get us there, but finding ways to get students onboard can be tough.

The Key is full of creative resources and strategies to help teens take ownership over their mental and emotional health, preparing them for life both in school and beyond."

**Amy Lauren Smith**
Health & Wellbeing Teacher,
Consultant and Education Editor at
Choices Magazine by Scholastic.


"The Key engages students to better understand their thoughts, emotions, behaviours, actions, reactions and how they interact with the school, their friends and with their parents at home. Romi's aim is to increase self-awareness and create behaviour change at home, at school and out in the world. Clearly the students changed from some negative thoughts to positive ones as well as treating their peers and parents with more gratitude. Romi has changed a number of students in a positive manner and I commend her on all that she has achieved."

**Ian Poyser**
Assistant Principal-Pastoral Care.
Head of Middle School Bialik College.


"Romi is a passionate and innovative educator who is dedicated to working with young people, helping them discover what motivates and engages them through the exploration of their own sense of self.

Throughout the duration of this inspiring 10-week guided program, I was fortunate enough to witness a group of young adolescents begin to question their personal choices - their words and actions, as well as the direct impact they can have on the lives of others.

The opportunity to acquire and develop such an authentic and honest self-awareness presented itself in a variety of ways, each session of vital significance and critical to the overall goals of "The Key." Students remained focused and keen to participate, sharing their thinking and ideas, which were encouraged, valued and appreciated by the expert facilitator."

**Soo Isaacs**
High School English/Humanities.
Teacher at Bialik College for 41 years,
Melbourne, Australia.

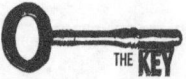

"Romi's book The Key is an engaging way to assist young people understand the complexity around dealing with emotions and coping in this ever increasing challenging world. The guided program is a perfect well being program for any school.

The program puts the young person at the centre of all activities. It helps them understand how they can be in control of their own responses to situations. The activities, videos and readings assist young people to develop life long skills - all of which they can take into adulthood, creating a more balanced, happy person capable of working through life's hiccups.

The three sections to the program target areas that impact on every young person. It provides insight into key strategies that have proven to support overall health and wellbeing. Gaining insight into who they are as a young person, encouraging students to focus on strengths and giving them the confidence to take on challenges is every teachers goal. This program helps to achieve this."

**Dr Louise Van Corler**
**(BA, BSW, MSW, PhD, Grad Dip Education)**
Director WeSupportU.
Teacher and School Social Worker, Melbourne, Australia.
Former Senior Lecturer in Social Work and Education at Monash University.

"I am highly impressed with this book and that it is being offered to young teenagers to benefit them, it's a big step for society. I'm thrilled that adolescents are learning more deeply how to think for themselves and working at something non-competitive, where there is no right or wrong.

When I assessed teachers, no one ever talked about topics such as 'tone of voice'. How brilliant to be looking from a meta point of view. I wish someone had taught me that and topics such as how to handle negative thoughts.

I think the most important lesson here is that young people understand that they have an active part in how they feel, that life/emotions don't just happen to them. Knowing you can influence this means it can be easier to deal with.

This curriculum, giving teens tools so they are not completely overwhelmed, should be for every young person, in any classroom, anywhere in the world. This is what life is about. Our main goal is to be happy and self-fulfilling - happy with one self."

**Silke Vroegop**
Former School Psychologist
and Dean of Students, Holland.

## STUDENTS OF THE KEY

"I became more myself."

"I learnt how to overcome fears and think about my actions before doing them. Now I feel more confident."

"I told myself I wasn't stupid and I started to believe it."

"I realised how much of myself I didn't know about."

"I now try to look on the positive side in life and not always the negative."

"When I was stressed I believed in myself and I felt better."

"I became more aware of the difference kindness can have and its impact on people."

"I have been able to make better choices."

"I can be myself. I don't need to hide anything."

"I realise my parents divorce is not my fault."

INTRODUCTION

"You're braver than you believe, and stronger than you seem, and smarter than you think."

CHRISTOPHER ROBIN
IN WINNIE THE POOH.
BY A.A. MILNE

# THE AUTHOR

My name is Romi and I am the author of this book The Key: A Social Emotional Toolkit for Teens.

> Sometimes it feels nicer to hear from somebody than read so here is a little 'Hello' video from me.

▶ **The Key - Video 01: Hello!**

So who am I? I am a qualified Social Worker with a Bachelor of Social Science, a Bachelor of Social Work and a varied list of certificates in topics such as depression, anxiety and Suicide First Aid. I worked in community health centres in Melbourne Australia in the area of homelessness, mental health and drug and alcohol. I was studying a Master of (International) Public Health when I was offered a position in Cambodia and moved there for almost four years in 2010. There I was the Manager of 'Tiny Toones' - a hip hop centre in the slums of Phnom Penh working with street kids. From little children to young adults we used hip hop and breakdance to teach them life skills whilst encouraging them to learn Khmer (Cambodian language), English, Math and Computer. These were kids with backgrounds of gang life, drug or alcohol addiction, loss of family and those from extreme poverty. I was fortunate to be invited to present on the TEDx Phnom Penh stage on my work in 2010. Watch here: https://youtu.be/h4Hvkh9R6RU

From there I moved to Thailand to write a book on my life in Cambodia, a memoir called 'Hip Hop & Hope, from the slums of Phnom Penh' that will hopefully be finished by the time you are reading this. I also started counselling adults again at a health and wellness resort near my new Thai home. Many of my clients there asked me, 'How can I take you home?' And so I wrote a book based on self-enquiry, self-awareness and journalling called 'The 5-Minute Guide to Emotional Intelligence' available on amazon.

As I write this teen book I am still based in Thailand doing individual counselling sessions, couples counselling, running workshops and courses. I also work online counselling adults and teenagers. My counselling style is 'holistic' which means we get to look at 'all of you' rather than just one aspect or from one perspective.

For more information on who I am, you can check out this video:

▶ **The Key - Video 02: Who am I and why I wrote this book**

So why did I then write this book? Because I know that I never learnt the skills I needed and the coping mechanisms to deal with life or to understand myself growing up.

From years of working with adults and teens I realised that most of us never learnt these things. We learnt maths and science and in some schools now even yoga and meditation but not things like how to deal with jealousy or what is anxiety and what to do if we feel stressed. I call them life skills. I also call this whole set of topics emotional intelligence. In this book you will learn a whole range of these types of skills and coping strategies so that life feels more easy and every time you have a problem or fear there should be something in this book that can help you. You can also get in touch with me if you feel you need more coaching.

Here is another little video on what is in this course.

▶ **The Key - Video 03: What's in the curriculum**

If you want to hear what some of my former school students have said you can hear their words in the next video:

▶ **The Key - Video 04: What teenagers think**

"When I was five years old, my mother always told me that happiness was the key to life. When I went to school, they asked me what I wanted to be when I grew up. I wrote down 'happy'. They told me I didn't understand the assignment, and I told them they didn't understand life."

**JOHN LENNON,
THE BEATLES**

# THE KEY

Did you notice when you opened this book, the words around The Key?
Let's take another look.

**THE 🗝 TO BEING YOURSELF**

**THE 🗝 TO AN EASIER LIFE**

**THE 🗝 TO GROWING UP**

**THE 🗝 TO THE *REAL* YOU**

**THE 🗝 TO KNOWLEDGE**

**THE 🗝 TO HAPPINESS**

**THE 🗝 TO UNLOCKING YOUR THOUGHTS**

**THE 🗝 TO SURVIVING IN THIS WORLD**

**THE 🗝 TO EMOTIONAL INTELLIGENCE**

The last one on this list you may or may not have heard of: emotional intelligence. You may see it written in its abbreviated form: 'E.I.' or 'E.Q.' Both are used but I prefer E.Q.

You also might know the term I.Q. (intellectual quotient) which is looking at how smart you are, how intellectual. There are lots of tests to see how smart you are. In the past, getting in to universities and getting jobs was always based only on your I.Q. These days however, people are more and more interested in your E.Q.; How well you understand yourself, how well you relate to others, how you handle stress and how well you work in a team. So the rest of this book will focus on different parts of getting to know yourself, which will ultimately help you increase and understand your emotional intelligence (E.Q.).

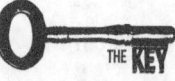

Throughout this book, I will be asking you to write answers to questions, put your thoughts down or circle answers. It is not a test. This is your own private space for you to learn and understand more about yourself. It is a space for you to challenge yourself. The more you get involved and the more you write, the greater your understanding of yourself will be.

This book is FOR YOU. So from now on when you see the key symbol 🔑 (the special key to unlocking your thoughts), you need to stop and write your thoughts down in the space provided.

## THIS IS NOT A TEST

Remember this is not a test and there are no right or wrong answers. It is for you to grow and discover more, through the three sections in this book: My Friendship, Me and My Family. There are tips, tools and learnings to be had in every section to help you better deal with life, deal with difficulties, understand sadness, happiness, challenges and discover the kind of person you are and want to be. So get involved, question yourself, discover yourself and have some fun.

We will stop for a moment here to practice writing when we see this: 🔑

🔑 **Let's write down what comes to mind when you hear the term 'emotional intelligence' (E.Q.). You read a little about it a minute ago but I want you to use your own words. Write at least two sentences.**

## EMOTIONAL INTELLIGENCE

Your E.Q. (emotional intelligence) is based on self-awareness. It is understanding your emotions and why you react to people or situations the way you do.

Increasing your awareness is important for the very simple reason that it ultimately makes life easier! It is difficult to notice the good or acknowledge the 'not so good' in life if you aren't aware in the first place. Understanding and increasing your awareness and learning some of the tools in this book can help you deal with pressure, anxiety, school life, friendships, relationships, arguments, family life and growing up.

✏ **Scribble some thoughts**

> "A real friend is one who walks in when the rest of the world walks out."

**WALTER WINCHELL,
NEWSPAPER & RADIO COMMENTATOR**

# SECTION ONE
# MY FRIENDSHIPS

# MY FRIENDSHIPS

Have you ever thought about what friendship means? When you think of friendship you might think of your *actual* friends names, most probably in a particular order.

🔑 **Friends, friendship, what does it all mean?** Write here the first five words that come to you when I say the word friendship.

1. _____
2. _____
3. _____
4. _____
5. _____

🔑 **Friends.com says that friendship is** *"a combination of affection, loyalty, love, respect and trust."* **True. Others talk about** *"emotional safety,"* **not having to** *"weigh your thoughts and measure your words."* **I like this. Think about it for a minute. Now write down what you think that means.**

_____
_____
_____
_____
_____

**I**s this true for you? Do you have any friends that you can completely and truly be yourself with? Or do you need to think and edit yourself before you speak? Do you do or say what is cool and what you're expected to say? Or do you say what you really think because you know it is safe to do so and that you won't be teased, looked at funny or told you're weird? Think about it. Be honest with yourself.

It's not exactly a lie when we say what we know other people want to hear, but it's not always the truth either. It is us trying to fit in, not stand out, be cool. We all do it. But wouldn't it be cooler if we didn't have to always concentrate or try so hard? If we could be honest with ourselves and our friends and know that everything would just be okay?

Being different or being called *weird* is not the end of the world. I personally think *that* is cool. Why should we all be the same? Wear the same clothes, share the same thoughts, always agreeing out of fear of not agreeing - the world would be a very boring place.

If all of your friends like shopping and you don't, then decide what you like to do and you can join the others later. Play a sport, join a club, go to a youth movement or find a hobby. Getting involved in activities outside school hours is a great way to open your mind to the world outside the classroom and your daily social world. Meet people from different backgrounds and different religions. Your school friends will still be there even if you leave for an afternoon to go to a hip-hop class, a football match or whatever it is. Those that don't accept your new activities are not true friends.

True friends accept all of your similarities *and* differences and respect your choices. True friends can agree to disagree without having an argument. So go to an art class, see a musical, learn how to play the piano, go to yoga, learn martial arts, join a choir, start meditating, play tennis, it doesn't matter which you choose. Finding friends, clubs or groups that support and encourage your interests and passions is important.

## ⟳ RECAP

**Circle which answer you think is true.**

**Emotional Safety is:**

1. Having to think carefully about what you are going to say before you say it.

2. Having to worry about what others might think.

3. When you can truly be yourself around your friends.

**True friends:**

1. Like you because you have a lot in common.

2. Like you including your similarities and differences.

3. Like you because you think the same as them.

## EXTRA CURRICULUR ACTIVITIES

Let's have a look at what you are or aren't doing already.

🗝 **Do you do any extra-curricular activities through your school?**  YES   NO
(Extra-curriculur activities are activities you CHOOSE to do outside of normal classroom time. E.g: sports, musicals).

🗝 **What activities?**

_____

_____

🗝 **Do the friendships you have feel different than in class?**  YES   NO

🔑 **How do you feel during (or after) the activity?**

🔑 **Do you do any activities outside of school with different people?**   YES   NO

🔑 **What activities?**

🔑 **Did you make any good friends there?**   YES   NO

🔑 **How do you feel during (or after) the activity?**

🔑 **List any activities you would like to do but don't yet?** (Maybe it's time to try one).

**Doing extra curriculur activities can:**

- Help me meet different types of people.
- Increase my social circle.
- Help me find like-minded people to connect with.
- Give me an outlet outside the classroom and home.
- Allow me to be more myself.
- Help me find and enjoy different types of hobbies and activities.
- Help calm my mind if I am feeling stressed.

**Scribble some thoughts**

> "My best friend is the one who brings out the best in me."
>
> **HENRY FORD,**
> **ACTOR**

MY FRIENDSHIPS

# WHAT KIND OF FRIEND ARE YOU?

**D**o you have any friends that you can completely trust to *be your*self in front of? More importantly, are you that friend? **Are you** the amazing and true friend that helps create that safety for your friends to be honest to you, without judgement, without editing, censoring or worrying that their thoughts might sound silly, weird or different? **Are you** that friend someone can tell secrets to without fear of you telling? Can someone confess to you their passion for a sport or activity that doesn't seem cool? Can they read you a private column they wrote? Tell you about an argument at home?

It is important to try to **BE that good friend**. Imagine how happy and calm the world would be if we were all that trustworthy, supportive, non-judgemental, non-gossiping friend. Imagine how safe and relaxed we would all feel to just be ourselves.

🔑 **So what kind of friend are you? Be honest with yourself.**
Write three sentences about the kind of friend you are when you are being a good friend. When you are at your best.

1.
2.
3.

🔑 **Now write three sentences about what you think you could do better or try harder at as a friend.**

1.
2.
3.

Below are some Yes and No questions. Again, this is not a test, this is just for you. Be honest with yourself. There is no 'sometimes,' so assess for yourself if it is *more* yes or *more* no.

| | | |
|---|---|---|
| 🔑 **If someone tells you a secret, do you keep it?** | YES | NO |
| 🔑 **Do you *expect* others to keep your secrets?** | YES | NO |
| 🔑 **Do you judge people by what they wear?** | YES | NO |
| 🔑 **Do you judge people by what they say?** | YES | NO |
| 🔑 **Do you judge people by who their friends are?** | YES | NO |

There is a difference between judging and noticing. We all notice what someone is wearing, saying or who they are hanging out with. We are only judging them when we form an opinion about it without wanting any more or real information.

| | | |
|---|---|---|
| 🔑 **Do you talk about your friends behind their back?** | YES | NO |
| 🔑 **Do you feel like you are the leader of your friends?** | YES | NO |
| 🔑 **Do you feel like an outsider with your friends?** | YES | NO |
| 🔑 **Do you follow what others say or do?** | YES | NO |
| 🔑 **Do you join in teasing someone else?** | YES | NO |
| 🔑 **Do you stand up for the person being teased?** | YES | NO |

Looking back at how you answered these questions, ask yourself this...

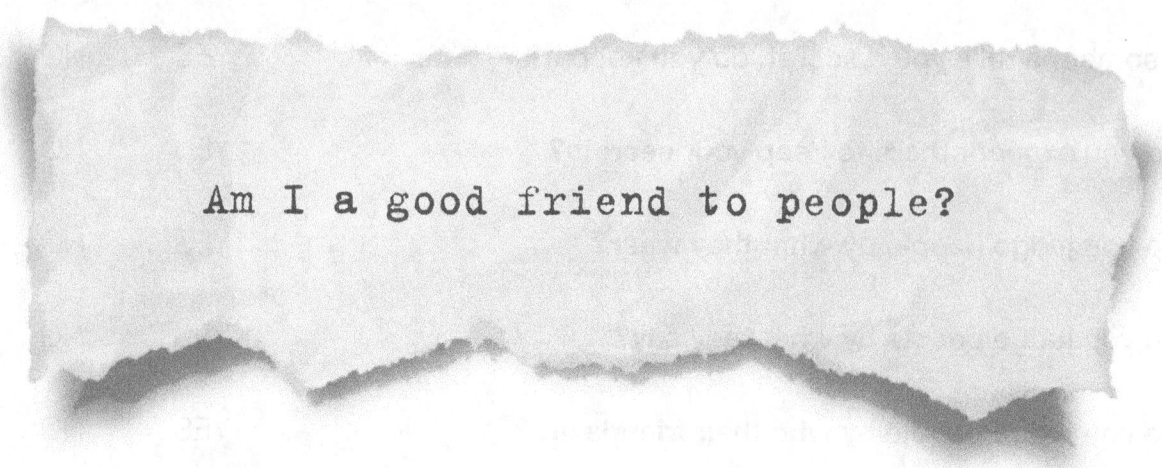

Am I a good friend to people?

If you feel confident that you are a good friend, then that is fantastic. Keep it up. If you secretly think that maybe you are not always a good friend, then it is worth thinking about what you can improve on.

Look at the three sentences you wrote about what kind of friend you are when you are being a good friend and the three you wrote about what you could try harder at to be a better friend. This is a great way to learn more about what kind of friend you are. You can then put it in to practice by doing some of the things you want to try harder at and doing more of the things you think you do well.

## ⚡ ACTIVITY - GROUP DISCUSSION

If you are in a class or group setting this is a good time for a group discussion. Share with each other in large or small groups the types of things you wrote on page 22 and how you answered the yes and no questions on page 23.

You can also share how you felt about having to answer those questions.

# BULLY CHECK-IN

Let's do a quick 'bully check-in'. Sometimes we can bully someone without meaning to and even without realising. Maybe we think it is a harmless tease. We can tease our friends sometimes because we think it is fun or funny. We say, 'we are just joking.' Sometimes we tease a boy or girl because we actually really like them.

It is good to just 'check' with yourself and understand when joking around can turn in to a person feeling bullied. The easiest way to check is to bring your awareness to the other person. Look at their face. Look at their body language.

`Here are a few questions you can ask yourself:`

- Do they look like they are having as much fun as you are?
- If they started off smiling, are they still smiling?
- Are they laughing with you or are you laughing alone?
- Are they starting to slowly step backwards? Wanting to leave from this situation?
- Are they starting to look a bit pale, afraid or like they might cry?
- Do they ignore you later that day or the next?

If you answer 'yes' to ANY of these questions, then even though you think you are having fun together, think you are doing some light teasing or joking, you are in fact bullying them. Make sure you always stop and do a 'bully check-in.'

**MY FRIENDSHIPS**

# STORY TIME

I want to share with you here a powerful story on bullying and bravery. I found this many years ago and it has the same impact on me today that it did when I first read it.

Below is 'Jared's story,' called: 'Each day is a gift'

Once you have finished reading, write down the first few thoughts that come to you.

## EACH DAY IS A GIFT
... and you never know how you can make the difference

One day, when I was a freshman in high school, I saw a kid from my class was walking home from school. His name was Kyle. It looked like he was carrying all of his books. I thought to myself, "Why would anyone bring home all his books on a Friday? He must really be a nerd." I had quite a weekend planned (parties and a football game with my friends tomorrow afternoon), so I shrugged my shoulders and went on.

As I was walking, I saw a bunch of kids running toward him. They ran at him, knocking all his books out of his arms and tripping him so he landed in the dirt. His glasses went flying, and I saw them land in the grass about ten feet from him. He looked up and I saw this terrible sadness in his eyes. My heart went out to him. So, I jogged over to him and as he crawled around looking for his glasses, I saw a tear in his eye. As I handed him his glasses, I said, "Those guys are jerks. They really should get lives."

He looked at me and said, "Hey thanks!" There was a big smile on his face. It was one of those smiles that showed real gratitude. I helped him pick up his books and asked him where he lived. As it turned out, he lived near me so I asked him why I had never seen him before. He said he had gone to a private school before now. I would have never hung out with a private school kid before. We talked all the way home and I carried his books. He turned out to be a pretty cool kid. I asked him if he wanted to play football on Saturday with me and my friends. He said yes.

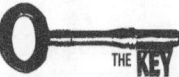

We hung all weekend and the more I got to know Kyle, the more I liked him. And my friends thought the same of him. Monday morning came, and there was Kyle with the huge stack of books again. I stopped him and said, "you are gonna really build some serious muscles with this pile of books everyday!"

He just laughed and handed me half the books.

Over the next four years, Kyle and I became best friends. When we were seniors we began to think about college. Kyle decided on Georgetown, and was going to Duke. I knew that we would always be friends, that the miles would never be a problem. He was going to be a doctor and I was going for business on a football scholarship. Kyle was valedictorian of our class. I teased him all the time about being a nerd. He had to prepare a speech for graduation. I was so glad it wasn't me having to get up there and speak.

Graduation day, I saw Kyle. He looked great. He was one of those guys that really found himself during high school. He filled out and actually looked good in glasses. He had more dates than me and all the girls loved him! Boy, sometimes I was jealous. Today was one of those days. I could see that he was nervous about his speech. So, I smacked him on the back and said, "Hey, big guy, you'll be great!"

He looked at me with one of those looks (the really grateful one) and smiled. "Thanks," he said.

As he started his speech, he cleared his throat and began "Graduation is a time to thank those who helped you make it through those tough years. Your parents, your teachers, your siblings, maybe a coach... but mostly your friends. I am here to tell all of you that being a friend to someone is the best gift you can give them. I am going to tell you a story."

I just looked at my friend with disbelief as he told the story of the first day we met. He had planned to kill himself over the weekend. He talked of how he had cleaned out his locker so his Mom wouldn't have to do it later and was carrying his stuff home. He looked hard at me and gave me a little smile. "Thankfully, I was saved. My friend saved me from doing the unspeakable."

I heard the gasp go through the crowd as this handsome, popular boy told us all about his weakest moment. I saw his mom and dad looking at me and smiling that same grateful smile. Not until that moment did I realise its depth.

Never underestimate the power of your actions. With one small gesture you can change a person's life. For better or for worse.

🔑 **Write down the first few thoughts that come to you.**

_____
_____
_____
_____
_____
_____
_____
_____
_____

## 🔄 RECAP

- Teasing, bullying or making fun of someone is not okay.
- A bully's behaviour says everything about them and nothing about you.
- Bullying is not healthy or balanced behaviour.
- For bullies to bully they need to feel bigger so they try to make you feel smaller.
- It is important for everybody to set their boundaries.
- Always speak to someone you trust if you are being bullied or teased in any way.

## WHAT CAN WE DO?

Firstly let's recognise that everyone, from little children right through to our grandparents, feels or has felt jealousy or envy at different times in their lives. Our first experience is often when a new sibling is brought into the family and we feel we have lost the undivided love and attention we were used to. Maybe our mum or dad gets a new boyfriend or girlfriend and we fear losing attention to them. Another common scenario is when a new student comes and joins our group of friends. We can be happy to have a new friend or we can feel jealous and worried we will be replaced.

So what are some things we can get jealous over? And more importantly how do they make us feel?

**EXAMPLE**

**Not being invited to a party can feel:**

- Like it is personal
- That people don't like us
- That we are being deliberately excluded
- Unwanted

**Having an older brother or sister can sometimes make us jealous because:**

- They get everything first
- They have a different relationship with your parents
- They are stronger, know more
- They can go out with friends until later or go away with them

🔑 **List three things you can get jealous over.**
How do they make you feel? What do they make you do?

1. _____
   _____
   _____

2. _____
   _____
   _____

3. _____
   _____
   _____

"Don't waste time on jealousy. Sometimes you're ahead, sometimes you're behind. The race is long and, in the end, it's only with yourself."

**MARY SCHMICH,**
**JOURNALIST**

# JEALOUSY & ENVY

**J**ealousy and envy have been around since forever really. Even Shakespeare (famous English playwright, poet and actor) spoke about jealousy and he was born in 1564! He called it 'the green-eyed monster.' Until this day green is considered the colour of jealousy and envy. These are terribly ugly emotions that cause unhappiness and no good comes from these feelings. So let's talk about them, let's understand them better.

Jealousy and envy are similar negative emotions and relate to comparisons (to other people) and competitiveness. Both can cause us to behave and do things we wouldn't ordinarily do. Both can make us feel insecure and feed anxiety or depression.

**The difference is most commonly explained as follows:**

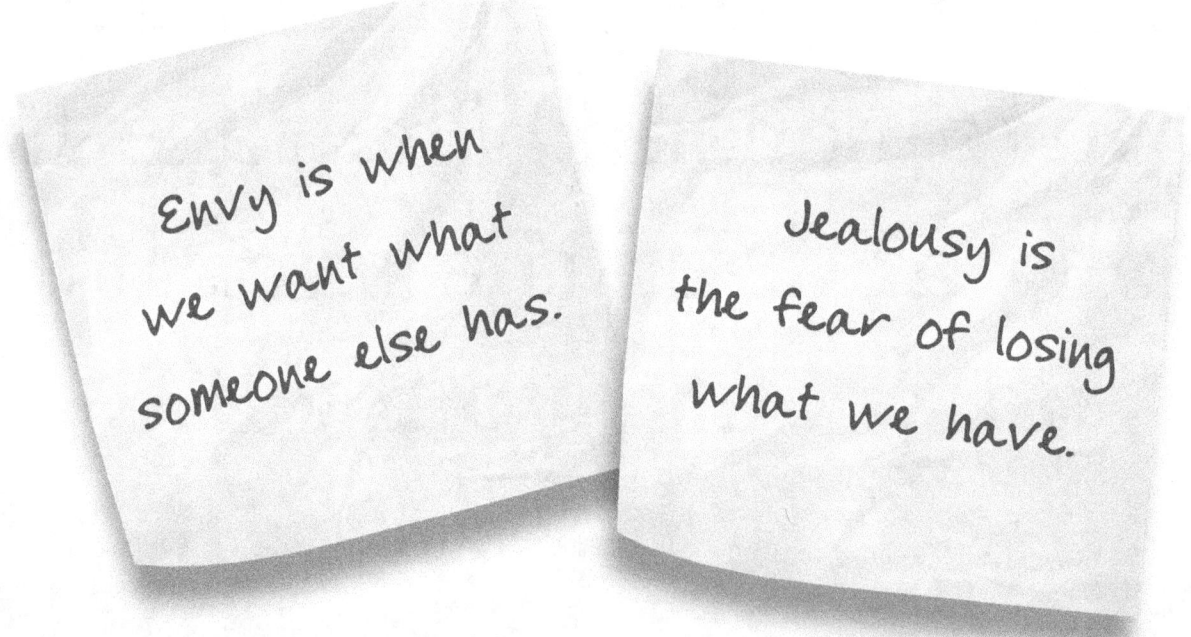

Envy is when we want what someone else has.

Jealousy is the fear of losing what we have.

For example, your good friend is going away on a family holiday with another friend's family. You can be *envious* of their holiday and wish you were going too (and maybe feel a bit upset or angry even though it is no one's fault). You can feel *jealous* that these two friends will spend all week together without you which may cause you to feel hurt, angry, left out, lonely and worry you'll be replaced in your friendship. Both can make you feel insufficient and insecure.

## THINGS WILL GET BETTER

Remember: A bully is NOT better than you, stronger than you or smarter than you. The words and actions of a bully can ONLY HURT YOU IF YOU LISTEN. Instead, listen to your OWN voice. If your voice (what you say to yourself) is stronger than their voice, then what they say will have no impact on you.

Remember that just because they said it (or wrote it somewhere) does NOT mean it is true. We will talk about this more in the 'Me' section on negative thoughts and positive affirmations. There, you will learn more tricks and tools to deal with this.

A little moment of truth: There is a reason I am telling you this about bullying. In my many years as a counsellor, I have met with thousands of clients who still hold on to the memory of being bullied at school. Years of pain and feeling bad about themselves. They didn't have the tools to work through it as a teenager, they never learnt the 'things you can try' that we just went through.

The reality is, years later as an adult, if you bump in to this bully who tormented you, one of two things is likely to happen. 1. They will be the one feeling bad, guilty and embarrassed about their behaviour, or 2. They will not remember you at all. So please, don't waste your time and tears on them now.

I have bumped into people I went to school with, some of the kids that were bullied and hated school and they are now THRIVING! They are in great jobs or loving university, have lots of friends and are really happy. All of them say the same thing to me:

> "I wish someone told me back then at school that things would change and get better. I wouldn't have spent so much time stressing and thinking my world was over."

So, I am telling it to you now.

**If you are being bullied, here are a few things you can try:**

1. Ignore them. If they don't get a reaction, they will eventually get bored and move on. They need you to react so they can continue. Don't do it. You ignoring them means you are not giving in to them. You are not giving away your power. No one has the right to take your power away.

2. Confront them. Be honest and upfront with them. No need to be aggressive, just take a breath and do it in a calm voice. Bullies may want to feel big but they don't in fact sincerely want to hurt you. Tell them what they are doing and ask them why they are doing it. Be strong in your own power. They are NOT more powerful than you, they are just louder.

3. If you have ever tried to argue with someone who will not argue back, you know it is impossible right? It takes two. So keep your voice calm and reasonable even if they are yelling or carrying on. Remain calm. Show love, kindness and compassion. They can't continue to yell if you remain in this state. They will look and feel silly. (If nothing else, holding this position will confuse or frustrate them, right?)

4. Don't take it personally. It is NOT personal even though it may sound or feel that way. If you are being bullied for having no friends (and maybe you do or don't), it doesn't matter, the point is the bully doesn't actually care. They don't care if you have friends or not and they probably don't know you well or care that much about your life - so it is NOT personal. They are probably terrified of losing friends or not being cool one day so are trying to stamp their authority on you to feel better.

5. If someone is teasing you and calling you stupid or dumb, it is not because they care how smart you are or what grades you get, maybe they are learning this behaviour at home or somewhere else. Maybe they are being compared to their sibling and told they are not as smart or their football coach looks down on them for not being as good. Their reason for teasing you has NOTHING to do with you and everything to do with them.

6. If the bully continues to bully, please go and tell someone - a parent, teacher, counsellor, aunty or someone. Remember you have done nothing wrong and you do not deserve this or need to put up with it. If the person you talk to does nothing, go and talk to someone else. Do not give up. Keep talking until someone listens. This is your right.

**E**ven those who seem to have everything, don't be fooled into thinking this is true. If they had everything (money and cool stuff doesn't count, I am talking about love, safety in the home, attention) then they wouldn't feel the need to bully, would they? Should we empathise with them? Feel bad for them? Some say yes, some say no. If you can, then try, even just a little.

To feel better, bullies need to feel 'bigger' and to feel bigger they need to make you feel smaller. It is not because you did something or look a certain way, that's just the excuse they use to make themselves feel good and sound smart. You know better! Don't give them the satisfaction of your reaction if you can help it. That's exactly what they are hoping for. Know that you are not less than them in any way.

## RESPECT

As the victim of bullying, it is important to SET YOUR OWN BOUNDARIES and decide for yourself what you will accept as innocent, fun teasing (and sometimes flirting) that has mutual respect, and what is hurtful teasing. What do I mean by boundaries? What is OKAY and what is NOT OKAY for you. That gut feeling of yours will be quick to tell you when something is *not* okay and when someone has overstepped the boundaries of what you are comfortable with and what you are willing to accept.

Here's another way to understand this. If you are playing basketball, tennis or many other sports, there are lines on the court or field that you can't cross. Maybe your foot touches the line but the referee doesn't notice so you get away with it. Maybe next time you put your foot a little more over the line, and again a little more. You keep pushing the boundaries until you get caught. We can do that in relationships and in bullying. We can push the boundaries and if no one tells us to stop, we can take it too far. Know when to say "stop" before it goes too far.

We are not always good at setting our own boundaries (even as adults). We feel uncomfortable and can think we are being rude when we just want people to like us. Even still, set your boundaries. It is not rude to know what you want. It will keep you safe. If something is not okay then it is not okay.

# BULLIES

Teasing, bullying or making fun of someone else is NOT OKAY. I know that sounds obvious and you probably all agree *in theory*.

> If you are the one doing the teasing or bullying, STOP NOW.

> If you are the one being bullied, know that you did nothing wrong. You did nothing to deserve this. There is NOTHING WRONG WITH YOU.

What is important to know straight up is this - it will NOT always be this way!

I know when you are being teased or bullied, it can feel like the end of the world. It can feel like this will always be your life. This is NOT true. It will not be forever. You will grow older (weeks, months and years) as will your bully, and things will change.

## THINGS WILL CHANGE

Even if you are being bullied about something that is actually true, e.g.: you're short or you're flat chested, the same applies. Things will change. You may or may not grow taller or bigger boobs but your attitude and others' attitudes will change. What you find important will change. You will learn to focus on all your amazing qualities and not on something as insignificant as height, weight or chest size.

Bullying and being a bully is not normal behaviour. It is not healthy behaviour and it is not balanced behaviour. People who are loved, happy, feel safe and feel secure, do not enjoy hurting others and do not tease or bully.

People usually tease or bully because 'they can.' What you may not know is that it comes from a place of insecurity. Being a bully is a cowardly act and a bully only feels strong when others feel weak. It is a type of coping mechanism for not feeling adequate enough, not feeling loved, noticed or respected enough.

"Darkness cannot drive out darkness; only light can do that. Hate cannot drive out hate; only love can do that."

**MARTIN LUTHER KING JR.,**
**BAPTIST MINISTER AND SOCIAL ACTIVIST**

Going through this book, we will look at these different aspects so that you can understand yourself and your emotions and issues around self-esteem better. There is no 'quick fix', it is a 'forever' learning process. In the mean time it is good to remember that there is enough love, happiness and success for everyone, it doesn't run out.

## THINGS I CAN CONTROL V. THINGS I CANNOT CONTROL

You can't always control things around you but you can control the way you react and respond. Have a look at the things you 'can control' and the things 'you cannot control'.

### ⚡ ACTIVITY - SHARE & DISCUSS

Discuss altogether or in smaller groups how you feel about the lists below and then see what you can add.

If you are going through this book or section alone you can still think about how you feel and brainstorm what you can add.

**Things I can control**
- My behaviour / My response and reactions
- What I think / How I feel / My dreams
- My goals / Who my friends are
- Who I spend my time with / Who I trust
- Learning from my mistakes
- If I act on feelings of jealousy
- Asking for help / Doing my homework
- My decisions / Being a good friend

Surrounding labels: How others react and respond · Other people's decisions · Others being kind · Death · Past mistakes · Who likes me · The weather · My height · What others say · Other people apologising to me · My skin colour · What others think · Other people's behaviour

**MY FRIENDSHIPS**

## CYBER JEALOUSY & SOCIAL MEDIA

ow often have you posted a photo or video of yourself in the classroom while listening to your teacher? At home on the couch watching television? While taking your dog for a walk? Eating dinner with your parents? Or simply doing nothing? Probably not very often.

Of course all the photos on all social media across the world are of people having fun, doing cool things and out with friends smiling. There is nothing to be jealous of, you do the same thing. We all take a whole bunch of photos just to get the right one where we look our best. It's just not *real*.

Don't, for one minute, believe that everything on social media is real or a real reflection of people's actual lives.

Social media is a highly selective and edited version of reality. As American novelist and poet Erica Jong put it,

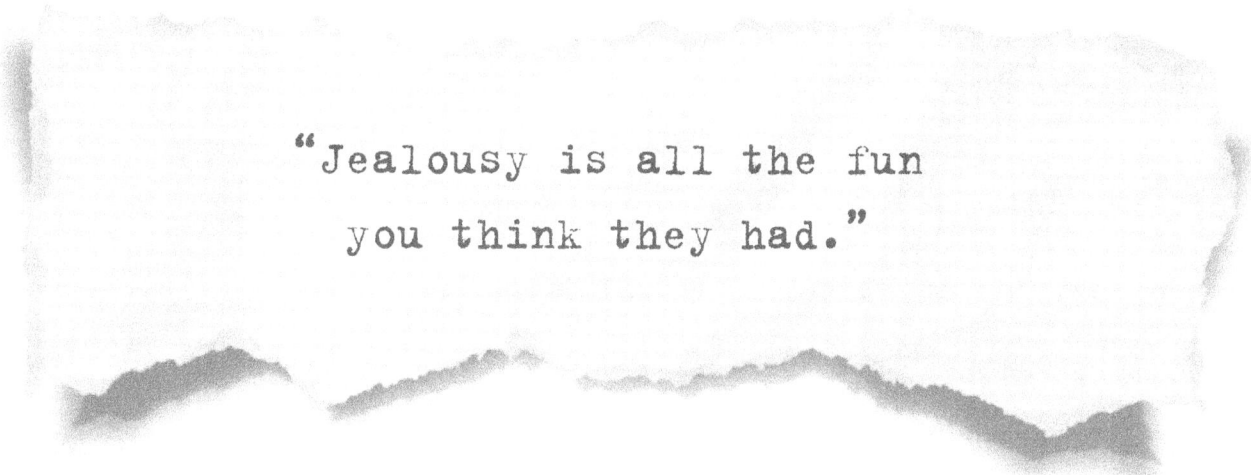

"Jealousy is all the fun you think they had."

The bottom line when it comes to jealousy and envy is how well you understand what you are jealous of and how you feel about yourself. The greater your self-esteem and feelings of self-worth are, the less likely you are to feel jealous or envious. You will have less reason to compare yourself to others because you do not feel you are missing anything, you feel good and happy the way you are and are more capable of being genuinely happy for others.

## ⚡ ACTIVITY - SHARE & DISCUSS

If you are in the class or in a group it is good to look at the answers you wrote to the above question and then share them with the group. Put all the things you came up with on the board so you can all see.

Discuss your answers and how they can make you feel.

We all have feelings of jealousy at times as you can see. It is how we understand it all and handle these feelings that matter. What happens when we don't manage this emotion? When we let it control us rather than us be in control? It can lead to feelings of:

- Competition
- Doubt
- Sadness
- Depression
- Anxiety

## ARE YOU FEELING JEALOUS OR ENVIOUS?

We would all like to believe that we don't get jealous but the reality is most of us do sometimes. It might not feel like we have control over it but we do.

**Read the next sentences carefully. They can help you.**

- Stop and recognise when you are feeling jealous or envious.
- Someone else's success does not take away from yours. Everyone reaches milestones at different stages of life and you will reach yours in time too.
- Remember what you are good at, your achievements and successes, to help balance out your thoughts.
- It is a good time to inspire yourself in areas you know you can worker harder in too.

MY FRIENDSHIPS

> "To live a creative life, we must lose our fear of being wrong."
>
> **JOSEPH CHILTON PEARCE,**
> **AUTHOR**

🔑 **Write here three different apologies you could have given but didn't.**

Pretend you are apologising now to that person (remember, it is never too late).
What do you think their response might be?
How do you think they might feel having heard your apology?
How do you think you might feel?

1.

2.

3.

🔑 **Write here three different apologies you could have given but didn't.**

Pretend you are apologising now to that person (remember, it is never too late).

What do you think their response might be?

How do you think they might feel having heard your apology?

How do you think you might feel?

1.

2.

3.

What do you find so difficult or scary? That it means you were wrong? That they will say, "You're wrong and I am right," or "I told you so"? If you are apologising then guess what? You probably were wrong. Just apologise when an apology is necessary. Keep it simple.

We ALL mess up sometimes, we have ALL made mistakes. That's okay as long as we remember to, and have the courage to, apologise.

A true apology is not just words but the meaning - showing you actually do care and respect the other person's feelings.

### When might we need to apologise?

- When we hurt someone's feelings.
- When we didn't keep a promise.
- When we yelled at someone.
- If we broke or lost someone else's belongings.
- If we were mean to someone.
- If we lied or broke a rule.

Can you think of any other times we might need to apologise?

### Good ways to make a genuine apology:

- "I am sorry."
- "I am sorry that I hurt you."
- "I apologise for not telling you the truth."
- "I apologise for hurting your feelings, I didn't mean those words."
- "I was wrong."
- "I will try not to do that again."
- "Will you please forgive me."

### Words NOT to use in an apology:

- "I'm sorry you felt sad or hurt"
- "I'm sorry but…"

# EMPATHY

**E**mpathy is sharing in someone else's feelings or understanding how they might be feeling. To do this we need to open our eyes to see and feel what is going on around us. When we talk to friends or siblings, or even our parents, check how they might be feeling. It is not difficult but does require our full attention. We can break it down in to 2 stages. 1. Notice what those around us might be feeling. 2. Respond to what you noticed.

Example: Do you remember a day when you were feeling down, maybe sad or angry and without telling anyone, your good friend noticed (Stage 1) and came to see if you were okay (Stage 2)? They spent time with you and understood your emotions. That's empathy.

🔑 **How do you think they noticed that something was wrong? What could be some signs?** Give examples next to each one of the following:

Body language:

Eyes:

Voice:

Out of character behaviour:

Gut feeling:

"Remember that the happiest people are not those getting more, but those giving more."

H JACKSON BROWN JR.,
AUTHOR

## ⚡ ACTIVITY - LEARNING FROM EACH OTHER

If you are in class then move to form small groups to sit with. Try and sit with different people than you normally sit with.

First answer the following two questions in silence and then share them with your group. This is a great time to ask each other questions and learn from each other. You can also come back together and share with the class.

🔑 **Can you think of an example, using the values you circled on page 48, when your actions or behaviour <u>were not</u> in line with your values.** What happened?

🔑 **Can you think of an example, using the values you circled on page 48, when your actions or behaviour <u>were in</u> line with your values.** What happened?

## ↻ RECAP

**Finish the following sentences:**

1. My definition of values is:

2. My top most important 3 values are:

3. These values are important to me because:

🔑 **Why do these particular values feel important to you?**

_____
_____
_____
_____

Values are often how you can measure what is going on for you.

When what you are doing is not in line with your values, you can feel like something is wrong (like gut feeling!). When how you live matches the values you consider important, things go along much more smoothly and you feel good.

**EXAMPLE**

If you value *belonging* but have done nothing about it, then you might feel lonely, left out and feel bad for yourself. If you do something in line with this value and join a community group or club, you would create that feeling of belonging for yourself and feel good.

**EXAMPLE**

If you value *health* but do nothing to make yourself feel more healthy then you will feel bad about yourself and probably guilty and feel something is wrong. If you did regular exercise, meditation or ate healthy, that would make you feel healthy and feel good about yourself.

**EXAMPLE**

If you value *intelligence* but don't do anything to expand your mind then you might feel bored, agitated and feel bad. If you worked hard at school, read books in your spare time, or had friends with similar interests to talk to, you would feel more intelligent and that would make you feel good.

# VALUES

🔑 **What are values?**

_____

_____

_____

_____

Put simply, values are what you consider important in the way you live your life. They stem from the lessons learned at a young age through parents, schools and community groups. We learn when we are little the concept of 'good' and 'bad', such as: *it is good to be kind and to share* or *it is bad to steal or lie*.

🔑 **Here is a sample of 44 values you could have in life. Circle ten that you feel are the most important to you.** You can choose to circle one from these below or add your own:

ACHIEVEMENT, AMBITION, BALANCE, BELONGING, CALMNESS, COMMUNITY, COMPASSION, COMPETITIVENESS, CONNECTION, CREATIVITY, EMPATHY, EQUALITY, EXCELLENCE, FAITH, FAMILY-ORIENTEDNESS, FITNESS, FREEDOM, FUN, GENEROSITY, GRATITUDE, HAPPINESS, HEALTH, HELPING SOCIETY, HONOUR, INDEPENDENCE, INTEGRITY, INTELLIGENCE, INTUITION, LOVE, LOYALTY, OPENNESS, ORIGINALITY, PERFECTION, POSITIVITY, PURPOSE, SECURITY, SELF-CONTROL, SUCCESS, TEAMWORK, THANKFULNESS, TOLERANCE, TRUSTWORTHINESS, UNIQUENESS & USEFULNESS.

OTHERS? _____

"Happiness is when what you think, what you say, and what you do are all in harmony."

**MAHATMA GANDHI,**
**CIVIL RIGHTS LEADER**

🔑 **Write here three compliments you could have given but didn't.**
What do you think their response might be?
How do you think they might feel having heard your compliment?
How do you think you might feel?

1.


2.


3.

# COMPLIMENTS

🔑 **When was the last time you gave a compliment? Did you mean it?**
Write about how it made you feel.

_____
_____
_____
_____

🔑 **How do you think it made them feel?**

_____
_____
_____
_____

`It is good to compliment people when you feel it necessary.`

If you appreciate, are thankful for, or are impressed with someone's actions or words, just throw a simple compliment their way.

`They will feel good and so will you.`

We often let those moments pass. Sometimes it is because we just didn't think to give the compliment even though it was probably a good idea, or maybe we worried that making someone else look good, would make us look bad. This is simply not true. In fact the opposite happens. Giving a compliment shows great strength of character and that you are confident within yourself and have a good awareness of others.

You can have empathy for any individual person or group of people, whether you in fact know them or don't know them. This leads to some much bigger questions around empathy.

What are you contributing to the world? It's a big question, isn't it? Maybe first we should try to define '*your* world'. For some people *their* world is simply their family and friends, for some it is their school, their community or country.

🔑 **What does your world include?**
Circle which ones you feel are part of the world that you care about.

FAMILY          FRIENDS          SCHOOL          YOUR CITY          YOUR COUNTRY

COUNTRIES YOU HAVE BEEN TO     COUNTRIES YOU HAVEN'T BEEN TO

YOUR RELIGIOUS COMMUNITY       YOUR SPORTING CLUB

COUNTRIES YOU KNOW FROM WATCHING THE NEWS          OTHER

What have you *personally* done for each of those that you just circled? It can be anything at all - something kind, spent time with someone that looked like they needed company, showed respect or appreciation, encouraged someone somewhere, showed love, signed a protest, stood up for someone, followed up on something in the news and planned to get more informed, raised money for a cause, donated your time for a cause, helped a friend who was feeling sad, or did something nice in your home.

**MY FRIENDSHIPS**

🔑 **What have you done? For each one of the ten you circled above, write what you have done.** We are looking for something you did without being asked, just because you felt you wanted to or it seemed kind or helpful. If the answer is nothing, then write nothing. Don't feel bad, we are all here to learn.

Family:

Friends:

School:

Your city:

Your country:

Countries you have been to:

Countries you haven't been to:

Your religious community:

Your sporting club:

Countries you know from watching the news:

Other:

## BEING PRESENT

To contribute to the world we must *be present* in it. To be present is to be aware in the here and now. You must be aware of other peoples' passions, pains, struggles and fights, not just your own. Living in your own bubble doesn't help anyone. The first step is to *actually* care and the second is to *act on* that care.

Caring about others' feelings and sensing others' emotions - this is called empathy. This is particularly important right now in the world with so much anger, trauma and horrible news going on. You might feel that it is not your problem, that you can't do anything or that the world's problems are too big. Not true. Everyone can do something.

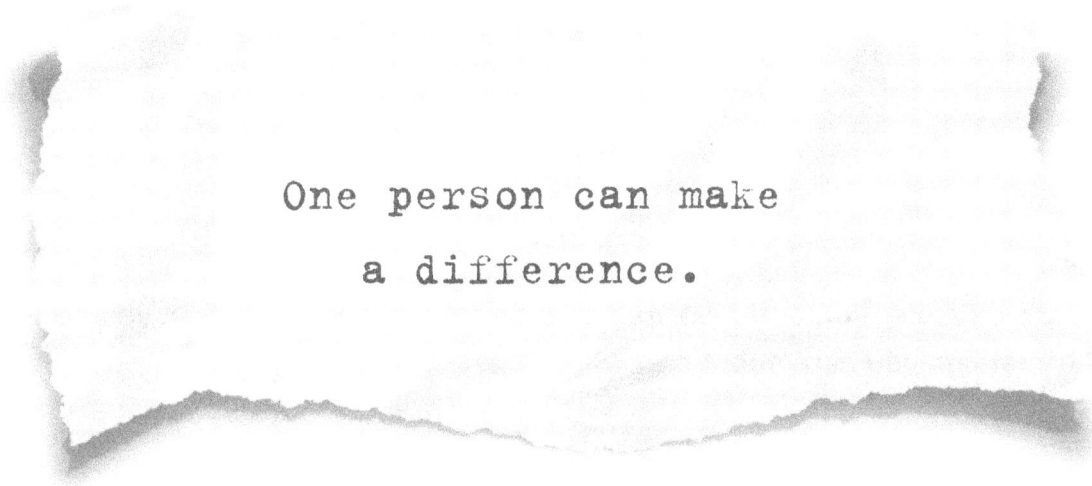

Maybe phone your grandmother or volunteer to visit an old age home and give someone company for half an hour. You can donate clothes to those less fortunate than you, help your sports teacher carry their equipment so they don't have to beg for volunteers or share a post on social media that is positive and makes people feel good, that helps someone in some way.

Don't do it for the recognition. Do it because it is the right thing to do. Do it because you are a good person. Being helpful, being caring, doing things, small or big, for someone other than yourself, should be a part of your daily life.

🔑 **What can you do for a family member this week?**

1. _____

2. _____

🔑 **What can you do for a friend or someone that you know this week?**

1. _____

2. _____

🔑 **Is there a cause or something in your city, country or the world that you could do? Something you care about and want to help with?**

_____

_____

🔑 **Why did you choose this particular thing?**

_____

_____

This is all linked to what kind of person you are and want to be. It is also linked to what kind of friend you are and want to be and what kind of friends you want to have in your life. It is worth stopping to think about.

# 'MY FRIENDSHIPS' WRAP UP

This is the end of Section One, which focused on

**'FRIENDSHIP'**

In Section Two, we will focus more on

**'ME'**

In this section we covered friendship, what kind of friend you are, bullying and the bully check-in, jealousy and envy, apologies, compliments, values and empathy.

When you are alone, have a look back at ALL of your answers in Section One. There are clues in here as to what kind of person you are and what kind of friend you are. It is important to recognise these aspects of yourself. See what you smile about, feel proud of, and know where you may need to improve or alter your behaviour. Take action if you need to. It is never too late.

If any of the topics in 'My Friendship' made you worry or confused and you want to talk to a counsellor (counsellor, social worker, psychologist etc.) about it then please make sure you do. But before you do, watch my video here about why getting a new counsellor is like shopping for shoes!

▶ **The Key - Video 05: Finding a Counsellor is like shopping for shoes**

"You have to trust in something - your gut, destiny, life, karma, whatever. This approach has never let me down, and it has made all the difference in my life."

**STEVE JOBS,
ENTREPRENEUR & CO-FOUNDER OF APPLE**

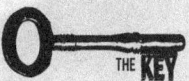

# SECTION TWO
# ME

# ME

🗝 **How would you describe yourself?**

Rate in order from 1 (most prominent) to 12 (least obvious). If you are not sure the meaning of any one of these words you can ask a friend, a teacher or look it up.

- [ ] SERIOUS
- [ ] FUNNY
- [ ] STUDIOUS
- [ ] HELPFUL
- [ ] CURIOUS
- [ ] KIND
- [ ] SENSITIVE
- [ ] EXTRAVERT
- [ ] INTROVERT
- [ ] FLIRTATIOUS
- [ ] SOCIABLE
- [ ] RESPONSIBLE

Now let's look at the different 'versions' of yourself. We will look at both the good and what can be improved.

🗝 **How would you describe yourself *physically*?**

_____
_____
_____

🗝 **How would you describe yourself *socially*?**

_____
_____
_____
_____

🔑 **How would you describe yourself *at home*?**

🔑 **How would you describe yourself *in the classroom*?**

🔑 **How would you describe yourself in *extra-curricular activities*?**

🔑 **How would you describe yourself overall *as a person*?**

## YOUR POTENTIAL

e can come across as quite different people in different situations. For example, socially I was popular and fun, physically I was quite tall and fit, at home I was rebellious and fought with everyone for a while, in class I was always told I "had potential" which I guess meant I wasn't really fulfilling it, and as a person I felt confused by all these differences. At 'extra-curricular activities' I was confident, strong and encouraging. I think this was probably my favourite version of me where I fulfilled my potential. Different parts of us shine at different times.

🗝 **Which version of you do you like best from what you have written about? Why?**

_____
_____
_____
_____
_____

🗝 **Which one do you like least? Why?**

_____
_____
_____
_____
_____
_____
_____

Now that you have thought about and written these descriptions of yourself, it is a good time to take action. If there are some parts of yourself that you really like and feel proud of, then try and bring more of this in to your life. If there are some parts that you don't really like, then maybe it is time to improve on those aspects of yourself.

## ⚡ ACTIVITY - MAKING OBSERVATIONS

Before I set you this week's homework we will try the exercise together in groups. Read these instructions first and then divide yourselves in to groups of 3 or 4. One person will stand in the front of your group and all face each other. Once you are all in position I want everyone in the room to close your eyes (your teacher can lead you in this) and stand quietly. Everybody take three deep breaths.

Open your eyes and look at just the person at the front of your small group. Those that are 'watching' the person, start to notice what things you like about them. Do you like their eyes, their smile, their hair or their skin? Do you like their intelligence, their humour, their story telling, their athleticism? From looking at them and from knowing them (if you do know them), what are some things you like about them. Try and come up with something different and then tell them one at a time. Remember to be kind. Remember to keep it positive. Remember you are next!

The person hearing these comments can say thank you or simply smile. Do try and keep eye contact though rather than look at the floor. I know it is uncomfortable but please try anyway.

Once you have gone around your circle, swap for the next person in your group to be the one standing at the front. Keep going until you have all had a go.

When you are all finished, share your experiences with the whole class.

Once you get to the homework activity on the next page, try and remember the positive comments you heard today to see if you can 'see' them too when you look at yourself.

## 🏠 HOMEWORK

I want you to go home and look in the mirror. Just stand there and look at yourself for one whole minute. See if you can stand still without shuffling your feet or fidgeting with your hands. Hold your own eye contact and forget about how uncomfortable this might make you feel.

🔑 **After one minute, write straight away what you physically saw when you looked at yourself in the mirror. What did you notice about yourself?**
Do it right away so the image is still strong. If you are feeling uncertain you can read page 68 and 69 first and then come back.

_____

_____

_____

_____

_____

_____

_____

_____

_____

_____

_____

_____

_____

🔑 **Then write how you felt during that exercise, whilst you were standing there (comfortable, uncomfortable, why?). What thoughts or emotions came up?**
Again, do it straight away whilst the feeling is still strong.

There is no right or wrong reaction to this exercise.

If this whole thing makes you feel uncomfortable, anxious, confused or scared it might help you to know that this is perfectly normal.

When I teach this exercise to adults I get the same response from them so if you can do a whole minute or even almost a minute then well done.

Why does this exercise make us feel uncomfortable or anxious? Because it IS uncomfortable.

How often do we just look at ourselves? We might check out our clothes, wash our face, brush our teeth and do our hair but we are busy looking at just that one aspect of ourself.

If we stop and look at ourselves, just look and do nothing else, it can be scary. Maybe we notice a pimple, or a scar, or decide we hate our hair or don't like our body. Maybe we just don't like what we see.

Often when we find something we don't like, we can stare at only that thing.

This is NOT because there is something wrong with us but more because we got stuck fixating on the negative.

With an open mind we can look passed that.

With a positive outlook on life we can find other things we like.

With strong self-esteem we can be okay with what is.

Try and look passed the things you don't like. Try and find the kindness in your eyes, the honesty in your face or the sweetness in your smile. Find your body type suits your personality or you hair suits your face.

Know your body shape and height might change, your pimples might clear, your hair can grow or you can cut it short. Know that things can change. Find one aspect (hopefully many) of yourself that you like. You will most likely notice your physical self first and then try and notice your personality and character traits too.

Now see if you can go back and try the exercise.

### ✏️ Scribble some thoughts

"Talk to yourself like you would to someone you love."

BRENÉ BROWN

# TONE OF VOICE

ave you ever stopped to notice your tone of voice? Do you notice others' tone of voice? Do you notice the tone of voice you use with yourself? Bringing your awareness to the way you talk can really help.

Have you ever thought that a simple misunderstanding, or massive argument, can start just by the tone of your voice? Let's see how it sounds using the sentence "Can you help me?" You can ask nicely with a soft tone and the response will surely be just as polite and helpful. Or you can yell and use a harsh tone that sounds more like an accusation than a simple question because you are already frustrated. Chances are nobody will want to help you at all. In fact, they will probably yell back and before you know it, you are in an unexpected argument.

## ⚡ ACTIVITY - ROLE PLAY

Let's role play the two different scenarios to see how this looks. We are going to need a couple of volunteers. One of you is going to be the school student and one the parent or carer.

**Scenario 1:** You are sitting in your room trying to finish an assignment but can't understand. You have been looking at it for ages and are feeling really frustrated. It is getting late and you just want to stop but you know it has to get finished or you will get in trouble. You know you should have done it last week but you didn't and now you are tired. You need help. You don't get up but yell out to your parent or carer from where you are sitting.

Discuss what happens.

**Scenario 2:** You are sitting in your room trying to finish an assignment and can't understand something. Even though you are frustrated you know that it will be more helpful to step away from your desk for a minute and take a few deep breaths. After this you walk across to where your parent/carer is, explain the problem and ask for help.

Discuss the two different responses.

From today on, I want you to bring your awareness to your (and others') tone of voice. Every time you go to open your mouth, start to recognise the tone of voice you are using. Once you have practiced this, you will find that this awareness comes quite easily.

## 🏠 HOMEWORK

Every day for the next week I want you to journal on your 'tone of voice'. Just write down every time you noticed your tone of voice and what you noticed about it. Be aware of your tone. Notice if there are any changes (good or bad) and write a few sentences each day about it. It will only take a couple of minutes.

**Day 1.**

**Day 2.**

**Day 3.**

Day 4.

Day 5.

Day 6.

Day 7.

ME

"It is our choices that show what we truly are, far more than our abilities."

**J.K. ROWLING,**
**AUTHOR OF THE HARRY POTTER SERIES**

# CHOICE

One word I want to bring up at this point is a word you all know - **Choice**. It is a very important word to remember. The words 'decide' and 'options' are usually not far away either.

I want you to think about these words: Choice, decide, options. Why do you think we are talking about these? Why should we care? How can our choices or the decisions we make enhance or limit our options and opportunities?

🔑 **Why are these three words important to understand?**

_____
_____
_____
_____
_____
_____

🔑 **What do these words - choice, decide and options have to do with your E.Q.?**

_____
_____
_____
_____
_____
_____

## SMART CHOICES

**U**nderstanding yourself better leads to smarter choices. Every day we make decisions. In fact, every day you probably make smart decisions both in school and in life. You put on a jacket during winter because it's cold outside. Smart choice. You could have chosen not to put on a jacket but that seemed silly, didn't it? Every day at school you choose who to hang out with, choose to go to class or skip class, choose to listen in class or doodle and dream away, choose to want to learn or to not care because you think it is dumb.

Then there are choices within all of these choices. You've chosen who you're going to hang out with at lunchtime, you also choose what you are going to say or not say, if you're going to tease someone else, stand up for them or ignore it altogether and be a bystander.

When you have homework you choose if you are going to do it, if you're going to argue with your mum or dad, choose what kind of attitude you're going to do it with (defeatist *I can't do this*, or optimist *I'm going to try anyway*) and if you're going to ask for help. Yes, this is your choice. Not mum's, not dad's, not any other carer. How you behave and respond is your choice.

We have choices every minute of the day. You can choose that school is stupid and homework is a waste of time, do poorly in exams and spend most of your life wishing you had made smarter choices so you weren't stuck in a job you don't like, earning little money and wishing you had more options. That would not be the smartest choice though, would it?

## GOOD CHOICES LEAD TO GOOD OPTIONS

Understanding yourself, your emotions and increasing your awareness of yourself leads to better decision-making skills. All of this leads to greater options later in life. You can choose to go to university, choose what subjects you like, choose what jobs you want to apply for and what relationships you want to have.

I know this all seems far away, but it starts now with how you handle yourself at school and at home. With smart choices, conscious choices, positive choices, life will feel easier, less pressured, less stressful and more fun.

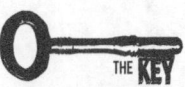

So how do we make good choices? How do we know? If you have a decision you need to make, whether it is big or small, how do you decide? Stop and think about it now. Think of a decision you had to make recently, whether it was to hand in an assignment on time or not, to tell your parents the truth about something you did, to go to a party on Saturday night or not, or which book to read next. See if you can remember how you made that decision. Did you ask a friend? Did you ask yourself?

🔑 **Which part of yourself did you ask? Did you do what *you* wanted to or what you thought you should?** Write your thoughts here.

It is important to understand how and where in your body you make decisions from. If I were to tell you that you can make decisions from your head or your heart, which one would you say you ask most?

🔑 **Circle one:**     HEAD     HEART

What happens a lot of the time when we're in conflict or confused, is we're having an argument between our head and our heart. The heart is our place of passion, love and desire, where we *want* from. The head is where we hold logic, reason and rationale. For example, you might need to decide between going out with friends or going to a tennis lesson on Saturday, between doing your homework or surfing the Internet. Maybe your heart is saying you really want to go to tennis today because you really love it, want to improve, have a hit with other players and have fun. Your head may try to negotiate and rationalise that you should hang out with your school friends so you don't miss out on anything or seem uncool.

As you get older, the decisions will get bigger so it is important to learn how to make smart decisions now. By smart I mean *listening to yourself*, understanding what you *really* want and remembering your values. Thinking again about it now, which do you listen to more - your head or your heart? Can you explain why?

🔑 **Can you describe why?** For the next two minutes, I want you to explain how you make decisions and why you think that is.

When your head and your heart are in conflict, you'll know because you won't feel completely confident about the decision you just made. It might put you in a bad mood or you might just have that feeling that something is wrong but you don't know what. So, the trick is to ask the mediator. I call 'the gut' the mediator.

## WHAT IS THE GUT?

**H**ave you ever sat down to a multiple-choice test? Do you remember circling an answer but later coming back and second guessing your initial response and changing the answer? You intuitively knew the answer straight away but were not sure how or why, so your 'thinking mind' butted in and tried to rationalise it until you concluded you must be wrong and changed it to a more logical sounding answer. Your 'gut instinct' answer is often correct. The trick is to trust yourself.

Have there been times when friends wanted you to do something with them but you knew it was bad or mean (stealing, lying or bullying, for example) and you instinctively felt a bit sick to your stomach or nervous? Maybe you said yes and went ahead but the whole time your body was trying to talk to you, to get your attention. You were feeling really uncomfortable because you knew, your body knew, your gut knew, it was wrong.

Your gut knows it is going against who you actually are as a person and who you want to be. Sometimes what you think you want (i.e.: to fit in, be popular, be cool) may not be what is best for you - that's why you feel uncomfortable. Try to look for those signs more often.

Before an exam you might feel physically sick in your stomach, these are normal nerves or anxiety. You also would know the expression 'butterflies in your stomach' which is excitement or happy nerves when meeting a cute boy or girl for example or before going to a concert. Again, that feeling is not in our brain or heart, but in our gut.

Are you starting to see that the gut is the centre of your emotions? Scientists and psychologists are now studying the gut and its relationship to our mental and emotional health and calling our stomach 'the second brain.' Let's not ignore or rationalise our emotions anymore. Let's understand and work with them.

 **RECAP**

**Finish these sentences**

Smart choices are:

Good choices lead to:

**The best way for me to feel comfortable and confident in my decisions is to:**
(Circle the answer you believe in the most)

ASK MY FRIENDS     ASK MYSELF     ASK MY FAMILY

## ⚡ ACTIVITY - OUR THOUGHTS, OUR CHOICES

On the next few pages are some CHOICES you need to make. For each choice there are positive and negative consequences. It is important to stop, think and acknowledge both before making a decision.

### 🔑 For each scenario answer the following.

1. Write down what might be the PHYSICAL positive consequences of your choice and write down the PHYSICAL negative consequences (there might be more than one for each).

2. Write down what might be the EMOTIONAL positive consequences of your choice and write down the EMOTIONAL negative consequences (there might be more than one for each).

You can do this on your own or in small groups and then discuss it altogether.

**Example:**

You almost failed your last test/exam and you have another one in the same subject this week but you don't understand. What would happen if you told your teacher you needed help and were scared because you didn't understand?

| POSITIVE | NEGATIVE |
|---|---|
| **Physical:** | **Physical:** |
| I might be able to understand and then study better. | Someone might see me and I might get teased. |
| **Emotional:** | **Emotional:** |
| I might feel more confident in the subject afterwards. | I might feel nervous or anxious. |
| I might feel more calm. | I might be embarrassed. |
| I might feel proud of myself for asking for help. | |

You will either decide to ask for help or you will decide not to. Your answer will depend on what you find more important.

A great way to make your decision is:

**Step 1:** Look at the answers you have come up with. This is the brainstorming stage.

**Step 2:** Feel your answer. This is the listen to your gut stage. Does what you decided FEEL right?

**Example:**

Your friend encourages you to steal a chocolate from your local store.
What would happen if you did?

### POSITIVE

**Physical:**

I get to eat a chocolate.

I get an adrenalin rush.

**Emotional:**

I might feel clever for getting away with it.

My friend might think I'm cool.

I might get popular at school.

I might think I can now get away with more.

### NEGATIVE

**Physical:**

Maybe I get caught and get in trouble

by the shopkeeper or they call the police.

My family might punish me.

I might get a criminal record.

**Emotional:**

I might feel a bit sick or scared knowing I

am doing the wrong thing.

Kids at school might be scared of me and

look at me like I'm are a criminal.

I might feel bad or guilty after.

You could choose to steal the chocolate or to say no to your friend.

A great way to make your decision is:

**Step 1:** Look at the answers you have come up with. This is the brainstorming stage.

**Step 2:** Feel your answer. This is the listen to your gut stage. What feels right?

**Now you try:**

**You have a test tomorrow but your best friend wants you to play an online game with them.** What would happen if you went online and played the game with your friend instead of studying?

| POSITIVE | NEGATIVE |
|---|---|
| Physical: | Physical: |
| | |
| | |
| | |
| Emotional: | Emotional: |
| | |
| | |
| | |

**Step 1:** Look at the answers you have come up with. This is the brainstorming stage. Write down what you would do.

_____

_____

**Step 2:** Feel your answer. This is the listen to your gut stage. Does what you decided FEEL right?

YES                              NO

**Your friends are all meeting together on a Saturday afternoon but you promised your mum you would babysit your younger brother or sister.** What would happen if you didn't meet your friends?

| POSITIVE | NEGATIVE |
|---|---|
| Physical: | Physical: |
| | |
| | |
| | |
| Emotional: | Emotional: |
| | |
| | |
| | |

**Step 1:** Look at the answers you have come up with. This is the brainstorming stage. Write down what you would do.

_____

_____

_____

**Step 2:** Feel your answer. This is the listen to your gut stage. Does what you decided FEEL right?

YES                              NO

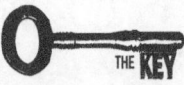

**You had a fight with your friend and you know that you upset them and hurt their feelings.** What would happen if you apologised to them?

| POSITIVE | NEGATIVE |
|---|---|
| Physical: | Physical: |
| | |
| Emotional: | Emotional: |
| | |

**Step 1:** Look at the answers you have come up with. This is the brainstorming stage. Write down what you would do.

**Step 2:** Feel your answer. This is the listen to your gut stage. Does what you decided FEEL right?

YES                    NO

**A classmate dares you to tease another kid in your class.**
What would happen if you did?

| POSITIVE | NEGATIVE |
|---|---|
| Physical: | Physical: |
| | |
| Emotional: | Emotional: |
| | |

**Step 1:** Look at the answers you have come up with. This is the brainstorming stage. Write down what you would do.

_____

_____

_____

**Step 2:** Feel your answer. This is the listen to your gut stage. Does what you decided FEEL right?

YES                              NO

"Pause for a moment, breathe, focus on the breath. Know that you are OK in this moment."

**LEO BABAUTA,
AUTHOR & BLOGGER**

# BREATH

**H**ave you ever stopped to notice your breath before? When you get a fright, you inhale and hold your breath. When you get anxious, you take short breaths, not quite big enough to actually fill your lungs and body full of oxygen. When you cry you can't breathe properly because you are gasping for air.

Can you see some patterns relating to the breath? Can you see how important the breath is to control and keep us calm? You don't in fact have to do anything to exhale, to breathe out, that happens naturally. What we need to concentrate on is the inhalation - the breathing in of oxygen because our body (including our brain) need it. It sounds obvious and you're probably thinking, "I breathe all day", but do you really?

If you have had a stressful day, if you come home upset, if you have an exam coming up, have a presentation to do, or have had a fight with someone, then lie down somewhere quiet and breathe. Start with one or two minutes and work your way up to five and more.

## TAKE A BREATH

**So why is it so important to learn how to breathe?**

Breathing can help us with:

- Calming down (it physically calms down our nervous system)
- Relieving stress
- Thinking clearly
- Focus
- Sleep
- Depression
- Anxiety

Let's learn different styles of breathing through these videos. You can try them all and use which ever one you feel works for you best or you can use them all if you choose.

▶ **The Key - Video 06: Learning belly breaths**

▶ **The Key - Video 07: Breathing with colours**

▶ **The Key - Video 08: Mindfulness Meditation**

Using this breath when you are upset, angry or confused will help you calm down and bring focus and clarity. To take it one step further, here is another little trick: Before you lay down to practice your breathing, grab a pen and paper and write down whatever is on your mind. Write without trying to understand it all yet, just write all your thoughts or frustrations. This will help clear the chaos of the mind. Then practice your breathing. This combination really helps clear the mind and bring calm.

**Step 1:** Write

**Step 2:** Breathe

If nothing else then every night when you jump into bed, take at least three of these deep full breaths. You will feel more calm, and ready for sleep. I still do this every night.

# ANXIETY

hat is anxiety? Anxiety is an emotion. We feel many different types of emotions all day long and that is okay. Like with any other emotion it only becomes a problem when it gets out of balance and we feel anxious more often than not.

Everybody feels anxiety at some point. We can feel anxious before a test or before we have to give a speech, try out for a new team or move schools. These are all perfectly normal times to be feeling anxiety.

People often ask if anxiety is the same as fear because they can feel similar. The answer is no.

```
Fear is when we worry or are afraid
about an immediate 'real threat.'

Anxiety is when we worry or are
afraid of a future 'perceived threat.'
```

The key words here are 'immediate' versus 'future' and 'real' versus 'perceived' which is more a thought, idea or maybe.

▶ **The Key - Video 09: Let's understand anxiety**

Watch this video to learn:

- What anxiety is
- When can we feel anxiety
- Where and how do we feel anxiety
- What can we do about it

🔑 **Then finish the following sentences:**

`Anxiety is` _____
_____
_____
_____

🔑 **Where in my body do I feel anxiety? How does it feel?**

`I feel anxiety` _____
_____
_____
_____

There are 3 steps I can follow to calm myself if I am feeling anxiety.

**Step 1:** I need to first…

**Step 2:** Then I can…

**Step 3:** Now I need to…

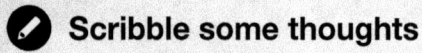# Scribble some thoughts

"Success is not final, failure is not fatal: it is the courage to continue that counts."

WINSTON CHURCHILL,
FORMER BRITISH PRIME MINISTER

# SUCCESS & FAILURE

🔑 What is your definition of success?

_____
_____
_____
_____

🔑 Give an example when you felt you succeeded at something.

_____
_____
_____
_____

🔑 What is your definition of failure?

_____
_____
_____
_____

🔑 Give an example when you felt you failed.

_____
_____
_____
_____

**H**ave you ever thought about the definitions of these before? Isn't it interesting that we can feel like we've failed or have a fear of failure even though we haven't actually defined what failing or succeeding means for us? It is not a matter of the dictionary definition but *your* definition. What is success for you? What is failure for you? It is important to remember to define these concepts.

Maybe your definition of success is having lots of money, the coolest technology or a big loving family.

🔑 **So what is success? Circle five of the following.**
   Again, these will probably line up with your values. Success for me is:

| | |
|---|---|
| DOING WELL IN EXAMS | BEING A GOOD PERSON |
| FEELING HAPPY | HAVING THE COOLEST CLOTHES |
| BEING FIT & HEALTHY | HONESTY WITH YOURSELF |
| GETTING THROUGH EACH DAY | FAMILY HAVING LOTS OF MONEY |
| BEING GOOD AT SOMETHING | HAVING LOTS OF FRIENDS |
| HAVING THE LATEST PHONE | MAKING FAMILY PROUD |

## KNOW YOURSELF

**I**t is important for *you* to think about what *you* consider success and failure so you know what you are striving for. You need to know for yourself when to celebrate and when you need to work harder. Maybe you tried out for the 'A' team in a sport but didn't get in, did you fail? Or did you do your best against some other very good players?

Your definition of success and failure can change depending on the topic and the stage of your life. For example, if you are very gifted at math then maybe anything below 90% makes you feel like a failure. If you find math particularly hard and don't understand it, maybe anything above 50% feels like success.

Other people's opinions can get in the way too. Maybe you got 80% and felt really proud until a parent said you should have gotten over 90% or maybe you have a brother or sister who always gets 95%, so you always feel like you're failing in comparison.

`True failure = not trying at all!`

> "I can accept failure, everyone fails at something. But I can't accept not trying."
>
> **MICHAEL JORDAN**

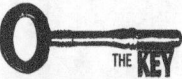

# ALL IN YOUR MIND

Is there something we can actually *do* to be more successful at things that are important to us? The great news is, the answer is yes! The biggest difference between success and failure is our mindset. Do you feel positive or negative? Do you feel calm and controlled? Can you see your success or is your mind focused on fear and failure? Your mindset plays a huge part in whether you succeed or fail at something.

**Here are a couple of strategies you can try.**

### 1. POSITIVE AFFIRMATIONS

On page 111 we will talk about positive affirmations as a tool toward personal happiness and unconditional love and you can use these same tools for success. You can design your own statements to help you recover from a perceived failure (by writing its positive opposite) or to move forward toward a goal. It will help you build momentum toward positivity, achievement and success. For example: Rather than telling yourself 'I am going to fail' or 'I can't do this', you would write down 'I am going to do well on my test' or 'I can study hard' or 'I am smart'.

Write them down and stick them on your wall. Surround yourself with positive statements and momentum toward success. It will help make you feel good and make you feel positive. Try it.

| What you might have said to yourself in the past: | What you could say to yourself instead: |
| --- | --- |
|  |  |
|  |  |
|  |  |
|  |  |
|  |  |
|  |  |

## 2. VISUALISATIONS

If you have ever read an autobiography or watched a documentary on a successful athlete, actor, musician or entrepreneur, you will see they all have one thing in common.

They do visualisations!

# Oprah Winfrey said, "You become what you believe" and made her way from extreme poverty to being one of the wealthiest women in the world.

Michael Phelps started visualisations in his swimming career at age twelve every night before bed and is the greatest Olympian in history. Actor, Will Smith says he saw himself as an A-list Hollywood star years before anyone even knew who he was. Singer, Katy Perry knew what she wanted from a very young age and put her visualisations on to cardboard at age nine when she made a poster of herself winning a Grammy Award, which, of course, she later won. I could fill pages and pages of stories of people who used visualisations to achieve success.

All of these people trained themselves to picture their race or routine from the beginning to their end success. Their practiced routine (the visualisation in their mind) became so 'normal' that they could be calm and feel fully prepared for the big day. We can do it too! You too can train your mind.

If you visualise in great detail, your brain can literally make new ways (a neural pattern) of thinking and when you repeat this over and over, it becomes habit so when the day comes, your body will naturally follow its set routine. If you have a big exam, a performance or a sporting grand final, whatever it is, visualise your day including the event being a complete success. Picture how you want it to go.

Close your eyes and breathe until you feel calm and focused. Picture your day feeling calm and confident with relaxed breathing and free of fear or anxiety. Don't worry if there are some nerves, nerves can be good adrenaline, but breathe through any anxieties or real fears. Picture making your way to the exam hall or sporting facility. See yourself smiling, breathing deeply, calm and relaxed.

Use your five senses as you walk yourself through the scenario to help it feel more real - What can you see? Is there a smell familiar with that place? What can you hear? How do you feel? Can you taste anything? Picture the first whistle or the exam in front of you and how easily you read through it carefully, taking your time and calmly, confidently answering each question all the way through to the end when you are sitting with a smile on your face feeling confident still. Picture kicking that goal or shooting that basket.

Start this visualisation technique weeks before so you have time to practice and for it to feel natural. Once you get good at it, you only need to do it for 5 minutes a day. You will find when the big day comes, you will automatically start doing all the things you visualised and will stay calm throughout the challenge.

> "In order to succeed, we must first believe we can."
>
> NIKOS KAZANTZAKIS,
> GREEK WRITER, POET & PHILOSOPHER
> (1883-1957)

"The greatest single cause of poor self image is the absence of unconditional love."

**ZIG ZIGLAR,
AMERICAN AUTHOR & MOTIVATIONAL SPEAKER**

# UNCONDITIONAL LOVE

As you grow older you may realise that other than your best friend(s), you have another best friend. And that is you. How does that make sense? Well, read on.

Who wants you to be happy always? **You.**
Who truly wants the best for you always? **You.**
Who is always there for you? **You.**
Who is the most able to give you unconditional love always, any time, anywhere? **You.**

Your friends and family can too, of course, but you will always be there, always, always without jealousy, judgement or condition.

If you don't already, you will learn to trust yourself and learn to love yourself unconditionally. What exactly does unconditionally mean? Not subject to any conditions or limitations.

 **Scribble some thoughts**

🔑 **Unconditional love for yourself or others can feel hard to achieve but it is really, really worth it. One good starting point is positive affirmations. What do you think they are?** Spend time now writing what you think.

To help find the right positive affirmations *for you*, let's first tackle negative thoughts to help us get there. So, flip the page to the next chapter.

"The darkness, the loop of negative thoughts on repeat, clamours and interferes with the music I hear in my head."

**LADY GAGA**
**AMERICAN SINGER, SONGWRITER & ACTRESS**

# NEGATIVE THOUGHTS

No matter who you are, how old you are, or where you live in the world, positive affirmations are a great tool toward personal happiness and eventually self-unconditional love.

There is so much negativity in the world; whether it is in your personal life or on the news, we're hearing negative words and phrases every day.

Unfortunately, a lot of us (almost all of us) have negative thoughts and voices in our heads. Everyone, at some time, hears these negative voices: *I'm not good enough*, *I'm not smart*, *I'm dumb*, *I'm ugly*, *I'm fat*, *I can't do this*, *I'll never have a boyfriend/girlfriend* or *no one will ever love me*. Does this sound familiar? We all do it. As kids, as teens and yes, still as adults. Look back and notice the tone of voice these phrases are all said in.

Sometimes the voice we hear in our head is a voice we know - a parent, sibling or bully. Sometimes it is our own voice and sometimes it is an unknown voice. The problem is that once we hear these negative voices frequently, it becomes a pattern and over time we decide (there's that word again) that what they are saying is true.

**Thoughts are not facts**. Let me say that again...

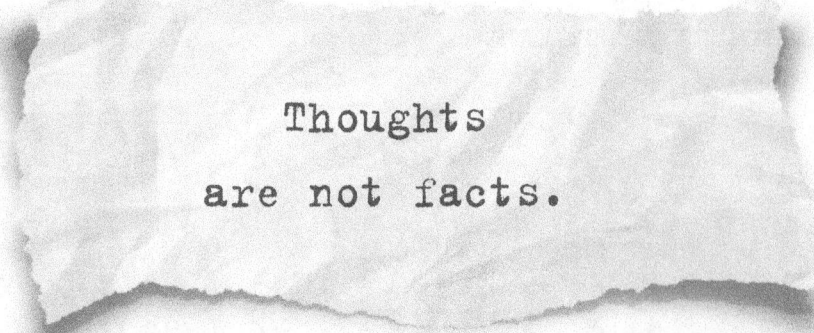

Let's better understand what negative thoughts are and where they come from.

▶ **The Key - Video 10: Understanding Negative Thoughts**

I will show you a little clip I made where I asked random people from all over the world the same two questions I will ask you:

1. What is the negative thought you hear?

2. Where does it come from?

Why did I do this? Because it is important that you understand that people of all ages from all countries can have negative thoughts or fears. You are not alone. Let's watch and hear what they have to say.

▶ **The Key - Video 11: What are your Negative Thoughts?**

What is the negative thought you hear?

Where does it come from?

🔑 **Now I want you to fill out this page with *your* top 5 negative comments that you hear in your head every day, week or month.** Don't worry, everybody has them.

1.

2.

3.

4.

5.

I want you to see if you can hear whose voice is saying each one (who said it first) and write down who it is next to the phrases above. If you don't know, simply write 'I don't know'. But often if you try hard, you will recognise if it was someone else's voice.

🔑 **Are you surprised at how easy or difficult it was to write down 5?**

                                                          YES           NO

🔑 **Seeing this list in front of you now, does it make you feel sad? Does it feel somewhat silly? Have you switched off so as to not feel any of it? Are you feeling upset reading this? Or do you feel confused?** I want you to spend the next couple of minutes just writing how you feel right now. Don't think about it, just write. There is no right or wrong here.

We will deal with these negative thoughts in the next section, I promise - where we create positive affirmations from negative thoughts.

"Once you replace negative thoughts with positive ones, you'll start having positive results."

**WILLIE NELSON,
MUSICIAN**

# CREATING POSITIVE AFFIRMATIONS

Turning negative thoughts into positive affirmations is a 4-step process that we will go through together bit by bit.

I have been teaching adults to let go of the negative voices that they had since they were your age. Don't hold on to these negative thoughts that are simply not true. Don't keep them for the next twenty years. Learn this process with me. Learn today.

Let's go through your list of five negative thoughts from the previous page, one at a time. We're going to rewrite each negative sentence into a positive sentence. We will remove all negative words such as 'can't', 'don't' and 'not'. Basically, we are going to now write what you *want* to hear instead. For example, if the negative statement is *I am fat*, then, rather than saying *I am not fat* because that sentence is still using a negative word, you would write any variation of *I am slim*, *I am the perfect weight for me*, *I am beautiful the way I am*, or *I am gorgeous*.

The point is to write what you want to hear, what would make you smile. These are your positive affirmations.

The ones that make you the most uncomfortable (because it feels scary) are usually the ones that you need to hear the most.

ME

🔑 **Spend time right now creating your positive affirmations and write them in the worksheet on the next page.** Keep the sentences short and to the point. It may take some time and does require your full attention. You can practice in the space here if you need to.

This stuff is serious and it seriously works but only if you do it.

🔑 **Now I want you to fill out this page with *your* top 5 possitive affirmations.**

1.

2.

3.

4.

5.

## TONE OF VOICE

**T**he bonus is that your tone of voice and body language will automatically change without you even having to try. We talked about tone of voice before but here I am referring to the tone of voice you use with yourself. Look back at your list and read out loud one negative comment followed by its positive comment.

What happened to your tone of voice for each one? The negative one usually sounds and feels heavy and like you're in trouble and the positive one sounds more gentle, loving, reassuring or full of determination. I'm sure you immediately felt more calm or inspired and probably took a nice breath rather than got stiff, angry, upset or held your breath. Your body language will change too from being slumped (negative) to standing up tall (positive).

Let's watch this short video on the relationship between negative and positive language, your tone of voice, your body language and the way this can all make you feel.

▶ **The Key - Video 12: Tone of Voice**

You have already identified the negative thoughts in your head and learnt how to re-write them into positive sentences. Now I am going to teach you the 4-step process to changing negative thoughts in to positive affirmations. There is a video at the end to show you how it looks.

## 4-STEP PROCESS

`STEP 1: AWARENESS`

Awareness is key. You need to start bringing your awareness to hearing when these negative thoughts arise. It might be a few times a day or occasionally. Start to notice every time you hear something negative in your head. You can't change things if you fail to notice them.

`STEP 2: TRAIN THE PUPPY`

Have you ever trained a puppy or seen someone train a puppy? What do they do when the puppy does something naughty? They use a stern voice that is abrupt and 'shocks' the puppy back to attention with the word "no", "stop" or a grunt noise "Uh".

Every time we hear that negative voice in our head, we are going to do the same thing but to ourselves. Lift your hand and put it out in a stop sign way or point the finger and say the word at the same time. If you like colours and are good at visualising them, you can picture the colour red for stop also.

### STEP 3: SILLY VOICE

Think of a cartoon character or a character from an animation movie that is a 'silly' character with a silly voice. Someone you could never take seriously. Now say your negative sentence using *that* voice. Do it <u>out loud</u>. Did you notice what happened immediately? I bet you smiled or laughed. It is impossible to get upset or feel hurt when the voice you're using makes you smile instead. All the power of the negativity has now been replaced with a smile.

### STEP 4: POSITIVE AFFIRMATION

This is the moment you say your positive sentence out loud. Out LOUD.

`Take it in.`

`Feel it.`

`Know it.`

`Remember it.`

Now you need to actually start saying these positive statements. Every time you *hear* or *think* a negative comment about yourself, I want you to stop immediately and remember the 4-step process. If you are alone, you can do it out loud, and if you are with people, you can go somewhere quiet or do it in your head. Don't worry, no one will notice. Just like *you decided* that those negative comments were true or fact, you can change it so that *these new positive affirmations feel true and factual*.

Check out 'Nik' who bravely did the 4-step process for me on camera.

▶ **The Key - Video 13: Negative Thoughts: The 4-Step Process**

## HOMEWORK OR CLASS ART TIME

Take your list and write out your positive affirmations using nice colours and stickers, making them cool, bold or pretty, cutting pieces of small paper so you have a bunch of them. If you're feeling brave, you can do this on a weekend with some friends so it's more fun. Stick them in your bedroom, inside your wardrobe, on the mirror in the bathroom, or anywhere else that you spend time in. This helps overwhelm your mind with positive comments rather than the negative comments you may have been used to.

*I LOVE you*

*I am Strong*

*♡ I am Beautiful*

*I'm a Good Person*

*I can do Anything!*

*I WILL pass my Exams*

Imagine every time you come home that your environment is filled with positive affirmations that seep into your mind and brain until they become your new norm and your new way of looking at yourself.

🔑 **Write a couple of sentences about how you think that might make you feel?**

The positive affirmations say whatever you need them to say. There is only one that must be added for everyone. "I love you". It might feel silly at first to read to yourself but loving yourself and knowing you love yourself is very important. You might hear it from family, friends or in relationships but the most important love you can receive is ultimately from yourself. Put this one on your mirror if you can. When you are checking yourself out, read it and say it out loud. Every day. You will get used to it and eventually smile rather than cringe.

"Happiness is not something ready made. It comes from your own actions."

**DALAI LAMA**

# SADNESS VERSUS HAPPINESS

🔑 **How would you define happiness?**

🔑 **Give five examples of things that make you happy.**

1.

2.

3.

4.

5.

🔑 **When you're not feeling happy, what does it make you want to do?**
(want to be alone, cry, get grumpy etc.)

🔑 **How long does your unhappiness usually last for?** (Circle one)

UNDER ONE HOUR    A FEW HOURS    ALL DAY    A FEW DAYS    MORE/LONGER

🔑 **Do you know how to 'get happy'?**    YES    NO    DON'T KNOW

🔑 **How would you describe this feeling of sadness?**

_____

_____

🔑 **Give 5 examples of things that make you sad.**

1. _____

2. _____

3. _____

4. _____

5. _____

🔑 **Of the 5 things that make you sad, are there any common themes between them?** What are they?

_____

_____

_____

It is important you know what can help you 'get happy.' This just means knowing what makes you feel good. It is totally okay to feel sad as long as this feeling doesn't stay for days at a time. If you know what makes you feel good, then you have something you can do for yourself. Some people find fresh air, going for a walk, run or swim, writing in a diary, talking to someone they trust or listening to their favourite song makes them feel good.

🔑 **Write here three things that you know make you feel good.**

1. 
2. 
3. 

🔑 **Is there a difference between sadness and depression?**

                            YES    NO    NOT SURE

🔑 **How would you define depression?**




🔑 **Have you ever felt depressed?**    YES    NO

🔑 **If yes, how do you know you are depressed?**
(if you answered no above, what do you think the answer might be)?


🔑 **How often do you feel depressed?** (Circle one)

AT LEAST ONCE A WEEK    ONCE A MONTH    EVERY YEAR OR SO    NEVER

ME

🔑 **What does feeling depressed make you do?**
   (For example: sleep, cry, want to hurt yourself)

_____

_____

_____

_____

🔑 **Do you talk to someone about it?**          YES          NO          SOMETIMES

🔑 **Do you start the conversation or do they?**          YOU          THEY

🔑 **Did you know that depression is on a sliding scale?**          YES          NO

🔑 **What do you think this means?**

_____

_____

_____

_____

 t is important to know that happiness is defined as feeling frequent positive emotions, AS WELL AS negative emotions such as sadness, anger and anxiety, just less often. You see, happiness does not mean 'not sad' ever.

Happiness, like sadness and depression, is on a sliding scale. This just means your mood levels can shift and change every day, week or hour, depending on what's going on. When you feel happy, you're sliding up the scale to the more happy end of the spectrum and when you're feeling sad, you are sliding toward the other end. Both are okay and no cause for concern. We move around the scale all day long. Depression is moving further along the sad end of the scale and is only a problem if you get 'stuck' down that end for long periods of time.

### ✏ Scribble some thoughts

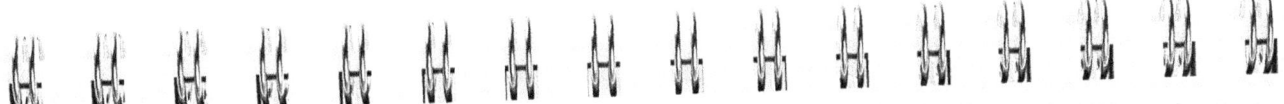

## EMOTIONS

We all feel a range of emotions. We *should* feel a range of emotions. Trying to suppress emotions usually just makes them feel bigger and harder to deal with. We can't be happy *all* the time and we probably wouldn't appreciate happiness without feeling the rest of the emotions we have. Do you remember in the movie *Inside Out* when *Bing Bong* lost his rocket and *Joy* was desperately trying to make him laugh and not feel his sadness? It took *Sadness* to comfort him and allow for him to have his feelings before he could move on. Let's watch 'Sadness comforts Bing Bong.'

▶ **The Key - Video 14: Inside Out - Sadness Comforts Bing Bong**

I also really like this clip toward the end of the movie called '*Sadness* saves *Riley'* where *Joy* truly understands and appreciates the different roles emotions play and the importance of working together with Sadness.

▶ **The Key - Video 15: Inside Out - Sadness Saves Riley**

Having an appropriate emotional response is the balance we are striving for. For example, it is normal to be upset or angry if a friend lies to you, just as you should feel happy or relieved if you achieve something you worked hard for. A full range of emotions is a good thing. Appropriate responses to actions is a good thing. Again, it is only cause for concern if you get 'stuck' in one emotion or when balance (under or over reactions) gets, and stays, out of whack.

If you are still unsure about what depression means or if you are worried you might have felt it at times, read the next page that describes it in a little more detail.

## STOP & THINK

What are some of the other topics in this book that you think might be able to help understand and deal with your feelings and emotions? Of feeling sadness or depression?

1. 
2. 
3. 

"Some days, 24 hours is too much to stay put in, so I take the day hour by hour, moment by moment. I break the task, the challenge, the fear into small bite-size pieces. I can handle a piece of fear, depression, anger, pain, sadness, loneliness, illness."

**REGINA BRETT,
AUTHOR AND INSPIRATIONAL SPEAKER**

# DEPRESSION

You, or someone you know, may have at some point in life, felt depressed. In this section, we are going to learn what that means.

The word depression can be used in a number of ways and is often used to describe how we feel. "Winter is depressing," or "That class was so boring it was depressing," or after a sad movie, "Now I feel depressed." After a really bad movie, we may even say, "That movie was so bad, I want to kill myself." This does not mean you actually want to kill yourself, you're using this as an expression of your mood at that moment. It's not a nice phrase at all but people do say it.

Like I said, depression is on a sliding scale and it is completely normal at times to feel depressed. If you are finding school difficult, having problems with friends, having issues at home or feeling confused about life for no apparent reason, you can feel depressed. This is okay.

Only if this feeling of depression is constant is this a problem. If it lasts most or all of the day, for weeks on end, then this is leaning more towards what is known as major or clinical depression.

It is important to understand what goes on during depression. Obviously, I cannot cover everything in this small section but I do want to give you an overview of the typical symptoms people can experience in *major depression* as listed in *headspace* (The National Youth Mental Health Foundation with centres all over Australia, www.headspace.org.au).

**Depression can affect you on four main levels:**

1. Your emotions

2. Your thinking and reasoning ability

3. Your behaviour

4. Physically

You may be experiencing depression if **each day** or **most days**, for **more than two weeks in a row**, you've felt:

- Sad and/or feeling like crying a lot of the time
- Irritable or moody most of the time
- You've lost interest or pleasure in your usual activities
- Feeling worried or tense most of the time
- Loss of interest in food or eating too much, leading to weight loss or gain
- Having trouble sleeping (getting to sleep and/or staying asleep), or oversleeping and staying in bed most of the day
- Feeling tired most of the time, or lacking energy and motivation
- Difficulty concentrating and making decisions
- Feeling worthless or guilty a lot of the time
- Wishing you could be invisible or disappear
- Feeling everything has become 'too hard'
- Being self-critical and self-blaming
- Having thoughts of death, suicide or hurting yourself

Don't freak out, we ALL feel some or many of these things at different times.

`It is okay. You are okay.`

**I**f you feel like this sometimes, this is okay. Look back through this book for the different tools that can help you. You can re-read the 'things to try' if you are being bullied, go back to the section on negative thoughts and positive affirmations to help move your mind and energy to greater optimism and self-love, you can practice breathing and go back to the YouTube clip on belly breaths, or look back on your definitions of success and failure to remind yourself how you feel about these. Something in this book should be able to help you through, with practice.

If you read the above list and feel that all or most of this is describing you and you feel like this all or most of the time for weeks or months on end, then PLEASE go and speak to someone. If none of this is news to you because you have googled depression before, maybe it is time to ask for some help too. Googling depression might be because you are worried you have depression.

There are helplines available if you cannot think who to talk to. Your school counsellor will know this too. Do NOT bottle it inside and try to do it alone. Remember, we all go through feelings of depression at some time in our life and this is okay. It is important to recognise them and recognise when it is time to ask for help.

If you read this section and felt that this did not really apply to you, then that is fantastic. The information here is to inform all of us. If you have noticed some or all of these symptoms in a friend or sibling, ask if they are okay. Recommend them to talk to an adult they trust.

# 'ME' WRAP UP

This is the end of Section Two, which focused on

`'ME'`

In Section Three, we will focus more on

`'MY FAMILY'`

'Me' is the biggest section of the book and may take some time to digest. You can come back to this section (or even this whole book) again any time you feel you need to.

We covered a lot of topics here; unconditional love, negative thoughts and positive affirmations, breathing, anxiety, making good choices, success, failure, happiness, sadness and depression. It's a lot, I know. But none of these aspects could be left out.

Make sure you fully understand the different topics of this section. Ask questions if you are not sure. They are all important in your understanding of who you are and who you want to be.

If any of the topics in 'Me' made you worry or confused and you want to talk to a counsellor (counsellor, social worker, psychologist etc.) about it then please make sure you do. But before you do, watch my video here about why getting a new counsellor is like shopping for shoes!

▶ **The Key - Video 05: Finding a Counsellor is like shopping for shoes**

"The bond that links your true family is not one of blood, but of respect and joy in each other's life."

**RICHARD BACH,**
**WRITER**

## SECTION THREE
# MY FAMILY

# 3

# MY FAMILY

Family should and hopefully does, truly have your best interests at heart, even on those days when you don't feel it. Your family should be the ones you can talk to the easiest, the ones you can trust, cry to, laugh with, or just sit in silence with.

**I** hope this is true for you but I also want to acknowledge that all families are different. Some families feel simply amazing to be a part of and this is great. Families also fight sometimes and go through all sorts of stages and this is normal. But there are also families that are abusive (physically or emotionally) or dysfunctional to an unhealthy degree. So from now on, when I say the word family, I refer to extended family, which means anyone *you* consider family whether they are blood-related or not.

Family now can include blood-relatives and anyone else you trust most in the world, those you would go to when you're upset as well as to celebrate.

Older brothers or sisters, aunties, uncles, cousins, grandparents, a trusted neighbour, teacher, family friend or counsellor can be great confidants. Finding someone safe to talk to is very important. If you are having a problem of any kind, talking to someone you trust is ALWAYS a good idea. Keeping it bottled up inside is NEVER the answer.

🔑 **What can happen when we bottle things up inside?**

🔑 **Now draw that feeling into a picture.**

When we keep everything bottled up inside we tend to go over and over the same scenario in our head, making it bigger and scarier than it was in the first place. Talking to someone can help put things back into perspective, give us a new perspective and give us an outlet to pour our emotions out in a safe environment.

Family (with the new definition of family), like all other aspects of life, needs work. The main thing to work on is communication. This will change and adapt as you grow. Communication plays an important role, especially going through puberty, school, understanding friendship, starting new relationships, discovering alcohol or drugs, and thinking about (or actually) kissing, touching or having sex.

*Don't forget all the things you have now learnt about your tone of voice!

From adults you can get *real* information, not unrealistic nonsense as in some magazines or online. Friends are great support and yes you are all in this together but to be honest, friends don't always know everything because they are also still learning.

Let's look at your family:

🔑 **Make a list of who, yes you can write their names, in your (extended) family, you trust.**

Looking at your list, think about the qualities in these people that you just listed.

🔑 **What is it about these people specifically?**
What qualities or values do they possess?

🔑 **How do they make you feel?**

🔑 Who in your (extended) family do you go to when you are sad or hurting?

🔑 Who in your (extended) family do you go to to celebrate achievements or breakthrough moments with?

🔑 Who in your (extended) family do you have the most fun with?

🔑 Who do you argue with the most?

🔑 What do you usually argue about?

## ARGUMENTS

If you have arguments often, try and think what they are usually about.
Are they 'real' arguments or over something silly?

A few things you can try to stop arguments from occurring or to resolve them are:

1. Listen to your tone of voice and see if this is adding to, or starting the arguments.

2. Breathe and calm yourself.

3. Stick only to the topic you are arguing about.

4. If you realise the argument is over something silly, stop and calmly walk away.

5. If you feel the argument is real, see if you can write about it from the other person's perspective. You may have a point but looking at the other side of the argument will help you understand their point too and help you to be able to resolve it.

6. If you know you have done or said something wrong, apologise.

"The ache for home lives in all of us, the safe place where we can go as we are and not be questioned."

**MAYA ANGELOU,
POET, MEMOIRIST & CIVIL RIGHTS ACTIVIST**

# MY HOME

Let's look at your home. What kind of *vibe* would you say it has? Rank from 1 to 10.
(1 = most predominant feeling, and 10 = least).

You may need to do it twice if you live between two houses.

🔑 **1st House:**

☐ RELAXED  ☐ STRESSFUL  ☐ LOVING  ☐ EMOTIONALLY COLD

☐ SUPPORTIVE  ☐ CHAOTIC  ☐ SCHEDULED/RIGID  ☐ FUN

☐ OPEN TO DISCUSSING ANYTHING  ☐ CLOSED TO DISCUSSING ANYTHING

🔑 **2nd House: if this applies to you.**

☐ RELAXED  ☐ STRESSFUL  ☐ LOVING  ☐ EMOTIONALLY COLD

☐ SUPPORTIVE  ☐ CHAOTIC  ☐ SCHEDULED/RIGID  ☐ FUN

☐ OPEN TO DISCUSSING ANYTHING  ☐ CLOSED TO DISCUSSING ANYTHING

🔑 **How do you *feel* when you're in the house?** When you leave your bedroom to enter the common space of the house, do you mostly feel (circle one):

**House 1:**  'CALM & PEACEFUL'  'WORRIED & STRESSED'  'DEFENSIVE & ON GUARD'

**House 2:**  'CALM & PEACEFUL'  'WORRIED & STRESSED'  'DEFENSIVE & ON GUARD'

🔑 **If you answered calm and peaceful, that's fantastic. If you answered either of the other two, can you explain why?**

_____

_____

_____

It's okay to try and talk to your parents about how you feel. Parents are people too and they may not know how you are feeling if you don't tell them. If this doesn't work or you don't feel comfortable, go back to your list of 'extended family'. Find someone outside the home you can talk to. It is important you find someone you trust to share your feelings with.

**Other things we have learnt so far that you can do for yourself:**

1. Practice breathing.

2. Practice positive affirmations.

3. Join an extra-curricular activity. Find people you connect with that make you feel good and help increase your self-confidence.

🔑 **Remembering our new definition of family, do you have anyone you can talk to?**

YES        NO        I THINK SO

It is very important that you do.

As a teenager, I talked to my older cousin. I also often talked to an auntie and my school convener. I was sent to a psychologist but I didn't talk when I was there. I felt uncomfortable, stupid and to be honest, angry for being sent there. My advice now, would be to try. If you have a bad experience with a counsellor or psychologist, that doesn't mean it's a bad idea. Maybe that person was not right for you. There will be one out there that is. Make sure you find them if you need to. Let's watch this quick video:

▶ **The Key - Video 05: Why finding a counsellor is like shopping for shoes!**

> "Divorce is probably about as painful as death."

**WILLIAM SHATNER,**
A.K.A: CAPTAIN KIRK, STAR TREK.
ACTOR, AUTHOR, PRODUCER & DIRECTOR

# DIVORCE

Let's talk about divorce. Maybe it has happened or is happening to your family or maybe to your friends or neighbours. It is quite common these days.

Being stuck in the middle of a divorce can totally suck. Some families handle it better than others, and many really struggle. Unfortunately, you can sometimes feel like the one caught in the middle.

Some parents may try and hide it from you, try and not fight around you and try to pretend everything is fine. You probably know better and can see through all of this and wish they'd stop treating you like a child. Know that they are trying to protect you in the hope that the less you see and hear, the better off you'll be. Some parents may just yell all the time. Even after the divorce they may still yell on the phone or when picking you up. They are probably still too angry to try to behave like a responsible adult or parent. Yelling, avoiding or horrible silences. None of these feel good.

You may feel split between two houses and guilty each time you are at one. You may be the centre of a tug of war and feel like you are a bargaining tool. You may not even know which one you can turn to or trust. Maybe one parent has left and never returned, leaving you with a bunch of unanswered questions.

You are not alone. I know this doesn't help but it is kind of nice to know that you are not the only one going through this, even though you may feel like it. Roughly 1/3 of marriages in Australia end in divorce, in the U.K. it is slightly higher and in the U.S. it is said to be up to 50%.

It doesn't matter which of these or other scenarios you find yourself in (there are many), what I want to tell you is the same. It is not your fault.

Let me say that again, it is not your fault.

If your parents are divorcing or divorced, I want you to say it out loud,

`"It is not my fault."`

Not only do you need to **hear** this,
not only do you need to **know** this,
but also you need to **believe** this.

Parents get divorced for all sorts of reasons and the reasons are between those two people. Nothing you did or didn't do could make your mum or dad leave or stay. Divorce may be happening around you, feel like it is happening to you, but it is *not* about you. Do not get involved if you can at all help it. Do not be the messenger between them. They are the adults and they will have to work it out.

## SHARE YOUR FEELINGS

what you need is to look after yourself. Find someone you trust to talk to, that extended family we spoke earlier about. Do not bottle it in. Share your feelings with someone you trust. I cannot stress this enough.

You may experience a range of emotions regarding your parents' divorce. There will be times you feel (or have felt) abandoned, worried, frustrated, angry, sad, stressed, guilty, relieved, protective over one parent or blame one parent, and a whole range of other emotions. It can be traumatising and feel overwhelming and exhausting.

Never ever feel guilty about any of these feelings. You are entitled to feel whatever you feel as you come to terms with this new family situation. It is important to try and not let the emotions that you are feeling override your daily life. For example don't let anger about the divorce get so out of control that you are always angry, maybe lash out and hurt yourself or others (physically or emotionally). This can happen if you are trying to bottle it all inside and have no outlet or person to talk to. The anger can take over. Just let yourself be angry in that moment. You have reason to feel angry. Breathe. Get your breath under control and talk to someone you trust.

Keep a journal. Write about your emotions and get it all off your chest. And again, in case I haven't said it enough, find someone you trust to talk to.

Exercise can also be a fantastic outlet for emotions.

Going through a divorce is likened to the same five stages of grief. Grief does not always refer only to death. Grief is the loss of any one person or thing and that includes a family unit. I will briefly describe the five stages of grief because I think it is important that you know this. Divorce can be a very big deal depending on how your family handles it. People go through different emotions and don't know why or what's happening to them.

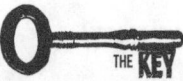

So, here I want to show you the five stages of grief: so whether you are trying to deal with a divorce, some other kind of loss (maybe a friend moved to a new country) or someone close to you died, you can use these five stages of grief to better understand your emotions.

**1. DENIAL**

"This can't be happening."

**2. ANGER**

"How could they do this to me?"

**3. BARGAINING**

"I'll study hard if they don't get divorced," or "I'll help around the house so they don't get divorced."

**4. DEPRESSION**

Sad, crying and not wanting to do the things you would normally do (school, fun activities, hang out with friends), "What's the point?" or "Why bother?"

**5. ACCEPTANCE**

Time to adjust. "There is nothing I can do but go with it."

It is okay to experience all or some of these, in any order. Let yourself experience them. If you get stuck in one, then you may need to talk to someone.

Your parents may behave differently for a while, whether it be sad, angry, quiet or in disbelief. They may want to spend time alone or overcompensate by spending extra time with you. They are also trying to adjust. They are also grieving. This has nothing to do with you. No parent gets married expecting to get divorced. They too will be feeling a whole range of emotions and in time, they will reach their own new normal, as will you.

As much as you might want to, you can't fix this. You can't fix them. You may want to run and hide or you may want to fix by helping more around the house, helping with siblings or being extra good and this is all fine but just don't overdo it. You need to take care of yourself too. Your job is to just be you. Nothing more.

# FINDING THE GOOD

So are there any positives that can be taken out of a divorce?

At the time, it might not seem like it but once things are a bit settled you may decide that everything might be okay.

The most important one positive outcome is this: **The home is now calm, free of fighting, free of tension and your parents are happier** - this is definitely a good thing. We all just want to feel relaxed and happy don't we?

You may end up with **two houses to call home** and that can be a good thing (and two sets of birthday presents).

You may eventually have **new brothers and sisters** or family and that can be a good thing.

You may **mature and grow up** faster than others your age because of the skills you've learned to adapt. You would have **learned a whole lot** about what to do and what not to do, for when you are older and in a relationship or marriage and learned how to handle yourself better. So, it's not *all* bad, is it?

# 'MY FAMILY' WRAP UP

This is the end of Section Three, which focused on

`'MY FAMILY'`

We don't often stop and think about our family, what it means or what kind of relationships we have with different members of our family. It is good to know who we turn to at different times and why, to look at our style of communication with different members and see where we can improve.

We covered some important topics here; communication, extending our family beyond blood-relatives, the importance of finding someone you trust, understanding your home environment, understanding arguments, divorce and even finding some positive aspects of divorce.

If I had to pick a topic here out of the list above to work on, I would say communication/ understanding arguments and extending your family to include all those people you trust so that you always have someone to talk to.

If any of the topics in 'My Family' made you worry or confused and you want to talk to a counsellor (counsellor, social worker, psychologist etc.) about it then please make sure you do. But before you do, watch my video here about why getting a new counsellor is like shopping for shoes!

▶ **The Key - Video 05: Finding a Counsellor is like shopping for shoes**

"Life is 10% what happens to you and 90% how you react to it."

CHARLES ROZELL "CHUCK" SWINDOLL,
AUTHOR, EDUCATOR AND PASTOR

# GOING FORWARD

Last bit of writing, I promise!

🔑 **If you think back through all the topics of this book, what are the three most important things you learnt?**

1.

2.

3.

on't forget to put your learnings in to practice. Even the topics that you don't feel apply to you right now, might feel more relevant in the future, so keep this book handy as your personal 'go to' guide for when you need it.

So, how do we conclude a topic such as this? How do we conclude 'The Key'?

**Does 'emotional intelligence' have an ending?**

There is no conclusion really. This is life and life is a never-ending journey of learning, growing and experiencing. So, whilst we are on this journey called life, let's make it the best we possibly can.

Let's choose to live in happiness, love and good times. There will always be things that annoy us, upset us, challenge us, hurt us and anger us. The trick is to know how to handle all of these situations. When we know ourselves well, our true selves, then the rest can play out quite nicely without too much stress. In fact, life can be enjoyable.

**Let's choose to be a good person, a good friend, and to make good choices.**

"I know where I'm going and I know the truth, and I don't have to be what you want me to be. I'm free to be what I want."

**MUHAMMAD ALI,
PROFESSIONAL BOXER
ACTIVIST, HERO**

# We have done a lot of writing over the course of this book. I hope it helped bring clarity on each topic as we moved through this course.

**J**ournaling helps bring focus to issues so you don't just drift through life without being aware of yourself and of those around you. If you enjoyed writing each week, don't stop. You can journal each day or week on any thoughts, feelings or activities in your life. It is private and for you only, without judgement. So start expressing yourself and have some fun.

This book was written to help you further know, understand and love yourself unconditionally. There are lots of practical tips and tools in here that you can practice and implement when you need to. You can go back to any section any time you want. Self-love is a life long journey, and a fun one at that. Don't forget your positive affirmations and breathing. This can help you get through.

The other thing I would highlight is be kind to yourself, listen and trust your own voice, trust your gut, your instinct. If your inner-voice is strong, then no one - no bully, no argument or put down, can hurt you. Know yourself. Trust yourself. Stand up for yourself.

Lastly, don't forget to extend your family to those you trust most in the world. Surround yourself with people that love and respect you and offer the same in return. Talk to them. Don't sit in silence. Share your pain and fears with them, let them hold you, share your love and joy with them, hug, cheer and celebrate with them and know you are loved.

If you think it might be fun for your parents to bring their awareness back to themselves and do some writing, remembering you are never too old or too young, then you can recommend my adult book to them: *The 5-Minute Guide to Emotional Intelligence*,
available on amazon and kobo.

# ACKNOWLEDGEMENTS

Writing a book is very much a solo activity. There are always people along the way though, that step up, listen to you, support you, brainstorm with you, offer advice or are just there for you as a friend and confidant. Whether their role felt big or small at the time to them, I am truly appreciative and couldn't have completed this without any one of them.

I would like to acknowledge the following people in no particular order - Soo Isaacs, Sandi Angel, Liliana Anichiarico, Demi Poyiadzis and Monica Forch.

To the brave people from all over the world who kindly agreed to speak their truth on camera in the hope they could save one young person from going through the pain they went through. A heart-filled thank you for you selflessness.

I also want to thank Bialik College in Melbourne Australia for inviting me as an *Artist in Residence* to teach THE KEY in 2017 and 2018. I thank them for believing in this program and the importance of teaching their students about emotional intelligence. As an author, I don't always get to share my books so deeply and profoundly with young people. I am honoured and privileged for the opportunity to work alongside the incredible teachers there.

Lastly, I want to thank Robin for his tireless efforts with the design and layout of The Key and for putting up with my constant editing and changing of mind, I couldn't have done it without you.

www.ingramcontent.com/pod-product-compliance
Lightning Source LLC
Chambersburg PA
CBHW060531010526
44110CB00052B/2571